London

Travel Publications

CONTENTS

INTRODUCTION

'When a man is tired of London, he is tired of life; for there is in London all that life can afford'. So spoke in 1777 Dr Samuel Johnson, the celebrated essayist and giant of London literary life. His words ring as true today as they did more than 200 years ago, for London can fairly claim to be one of the world's greatest capitals: exciting and lively, large yet highly accessible, and very much a human city.

The key to getting the most out of London is to appreciate the continual intermingling of past and present. In contrast with many other cities, London has never been subjected to grand master development plans – the city has instead evolved through constant but gradual change.

Each generation did, of course, build anew and impose its own stamp on the city – a process that continues still. London lost many of its historical sites during the Second World War, and some of the buildings that replaced them were sadly lacking in imagination. Many of these, however, are now being replaced with more pleasing ones.

As it did in Dr Johnson's day, London 'affords' every facet of a contemporary city: countless clubs and nightspots, shops of all kinds, from mega-stores to boutiques selling the latest fashions and art and craftwork, entertainments and exhibitions to suit every interest. But all this happens in streets and quarters that are

Trooping the colour

B. Morandi/MICHELIN

Big Ben

full of links with past Londoners, and mostly remain on a human scale.

The best way of getting to know London is to explore the city on foot. The six walks in this guide are designed to provide helpful introductions to some of the most interesting areas to explore. Strike off on your own whenever you want to – you will soon discover that London surely remains, to quote a writer three centuries earlier than Dr Johnson, 'the flower of cities all'.

■ Geography

London's history is inexorably linked to the Thames. The city was founded at the easiest downstream crossing-point, shortly before the riv er widens as it flows eastwards towards the sea. From the earliest days, travellers from the Continent would land at Dover and then follow the ancient routes through Kent to London. Meanwhile, vessels transporting men and goods sailed up the Thames to berth there. Importing and exporting, at first via the wharves on the river's north and south banks, then through the purpose-built 19C docks, be-

came a central part of London's economy. Only in the last quarter century or so has the city lost its docks, as new container berths with easier transport access have been constructed further downstream.

Some miles north and south of the city centre, two ranges of gentle hills, now mostly covered with suburban development, also help to define London. The city lies in a shallow bowl, which in summer retains heat.

■ History

Although the name London is of Celtic origin, the city only began to take shape under the Romans, who made it the hub of their road system, enclosed it with walls and built the first London Bridge. Remains of the Roman walls, together with medieval additions, are still visible in the street called London Wall and near the Tower of London.

It was Edward the Confessor (1042-66) who established the rival centre at Westminster, when he built a royal palace and founded an abbey, the minster in the west as opposed to St Paul's Cathedral, the minster in the east.

In fact London did not become the official capital of England until the mid-12C, as until then Winchester had been more important administratively. The City and its busy port gained considerable freedom and independence from the crown, which was often dependent on the City merchants for raising money for military expeditions. The City did not encroach on Westminster and, with few notable exceptions, citizens held no office under the Crown or Parliament but there was however much traffic between the two centres, originally by water – later by road. The great houses of the nobility lined the Strand along the north bank of the Thames and city merchants built elegant mansions in the less crowded West End or the villages such as Islington, Holborn and Chelsea.

The overcrowding in the City was somewhat reduced by the ravages of the **Great Plague** (1665), in which 75 000 out of 460 000 people died, and of the **Great Fire** (1666) which destroyed 80% of the buildings. Within six days of the end of the fire, Christopher Wren, then 33 years old, submitted a plan to rebuild the City with broad straight streets. It was not accepted and, although the authorities stipulated that the buildings should be of brick and slate, rebuilding took place round the tiny courts and along the narrow streets of the medieval city. Wren was however commissioned to build the new St Paul's Cathedral and the majority of the city churches, which demonstrate his great ingenuity in fitting them into narrow and awkward sites.

K. Brett/MICHELIN

Cumberland Terrace, Regent's Park

As the population continued to expand, the parish vestries, who were responsible for drainage, paving, lighting and the maintenance of the streets, proved unable or unwilling to control the proliferation of poor quality housing, to limit the increase in traffic and to provide sanitation. The appalling conditions of the 18C are strikingly illustrated in the work of **William Hogarth**; there are vivid descriptions of the poverty of the 19C in the journalism and novels of **Charles Dickens** and in Henry Mayhew's *Survey of the London Poor, 1850*.

Eventually in 1855 the Government established the Metropolitan Board of Works, a central body with special responsibility for main sewerage and to act as co-ordinator of the parish vestries. In 1888 the County of London was created with an area equivalent to the present 12 inner London boroughs. In 1965 it was superseded by the Greater London Council which controlled an area of 610sq mi/1 508km² containing a population of 6 700 000. In 1986 the GLC was abolished and its functions devolved to the borough councils and various new statutory bodies. Following a referendum of 1998, elections were held in 1999 and once again London has a new mayor as distinct from the

Chelsea Factory: the Music Lesson

M. Kitcatt

Lord Mayor of the City of London. The many bomb sites resulting from the Second World War (1939-45) provided opportunities for modern and imaginative re-development such as the Festival Hall, which forms the nucleus of the **South Bank Arts Centre**, and the **Barbican**, a residential neighbourhood incorporating schools, shops, open spaces and an arts centre. The most recent redevelopment project is the regeneration of the Docklands, several square miles of derelict warehouses and dock basins east of the City, north and south of the Thames, which have been converted into water sports facilities and modern flats, adjoining new low-rise housing and innovative office accommodation such as Canary Wharf. City Airport provides essential transport links to Europe. The townscape is changing as landmark buildings and other structures – such as City Hall, London Eye, Millennium and Hungerford Bridges – by eminent architects rise in the City

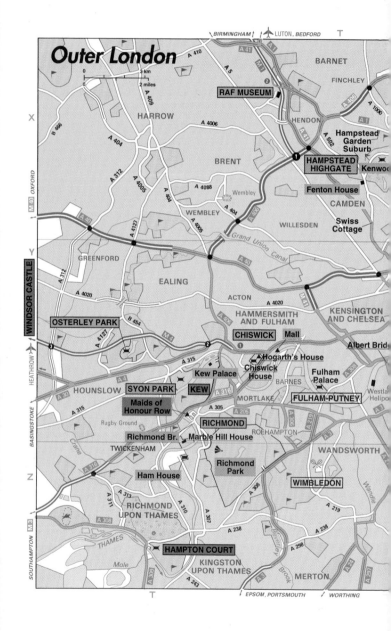

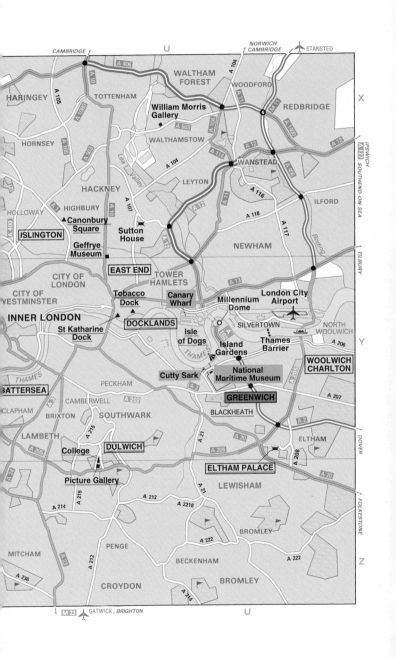

PRINCIPAL SIGHTS MAP

of London and along the banks of the Thames. In a bid to create a better quality of life in the capital schemes are being implemented to curb traffic, encourage more use of public transport and turn Trafalgar Square into a pedestrian area. It is also now possible to walk along the south bank from Wandsworth to Docklands.

Sword rest in St Magnus Church

■ London Today

The City, which is primarily a business centre and tended to be deserted in the evenings and at weekends, is gradually catching up with the West End, a shopping and entertainment area lively at all hours. In recent years the south bank has become a thriving centre of attraction.

Although few people live in the centre of London, many live in what was a belt of "villages" which have become completely absorbed into the metropolis but have retained their own particular character. It is worth exploring such districts as Southwark, Hampstead, Chiswick, Kensington or Chelsea to trace this evolution.

The cosmopolitan atmosphere of London has been greatly reinforced in the latter half of the 20C by easier foreign travel, higher standards of living, immigration from the Commonwealth and Britain's membership of the European Union, resulting in a more international outlook and an increase in the number of foreign restaurants and food stores. ■

Traditional London

Tradition still plays an important role in London life. The ceremonial **Changing of the Guard** at Buckingham Palace *(daily at 11.30am in summer; otherwise every other day)* and Horse Guards *(daily at 11am; Sun at 10am)* still draw the crowds. There is a fine display of brilliant pageantry and military precision when the Queen attends **Trooping the Colour** on Horse Guards Parade *(2nd or 3rd Sat in June)* and the **State Opening of Parliament** *(Nov)*.

In the **Lord Mayor's Show** *(second Sat in Nov)* the newly elected Lord Mayor of London proceeds through the City in the golden state coach before taking his oath at the Royal Courts of Justice in the Strand. The famous **London to Brighton Rally** begins with a parade of veteran and vintage cars in Hyde Park *(first Sun in Nov)*. A more recently introduced event is the annual **London Marathon** *(third week in Apr)*, in which thousands compete, running from Greenwich to Westminster Bridge along streets lined with tens of thousands shouting their support.

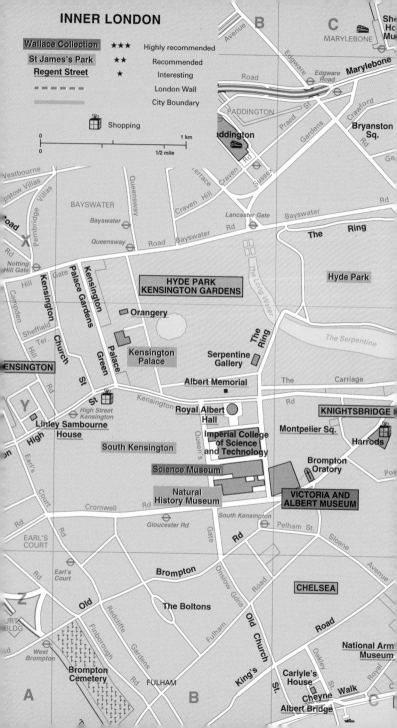

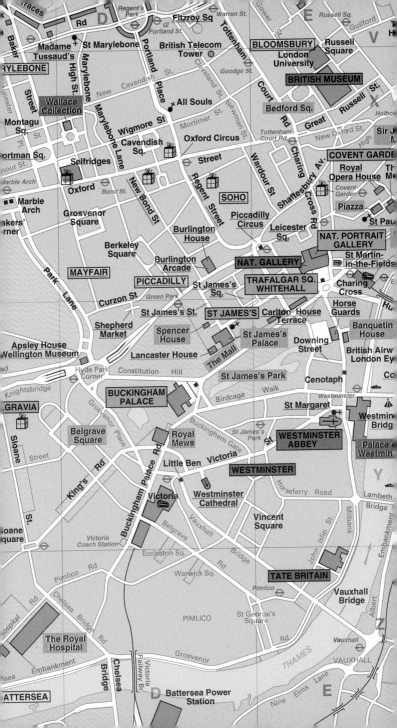

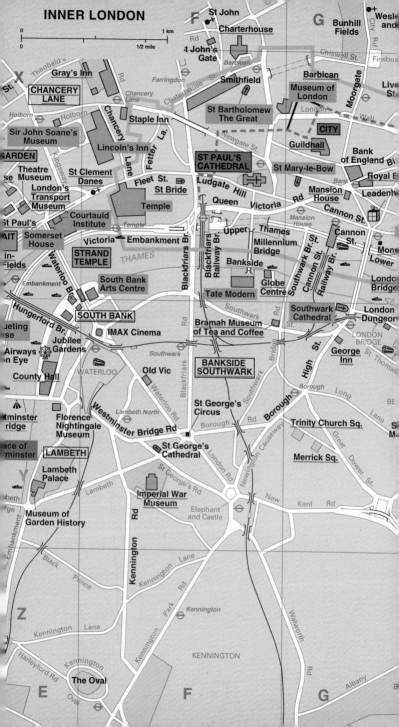

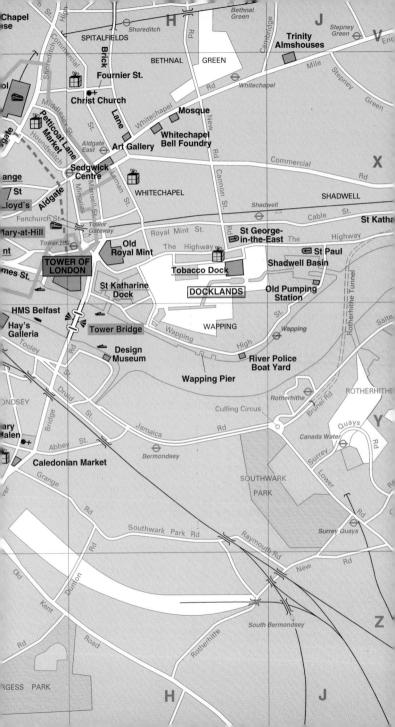

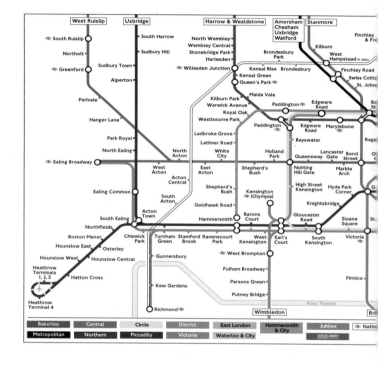

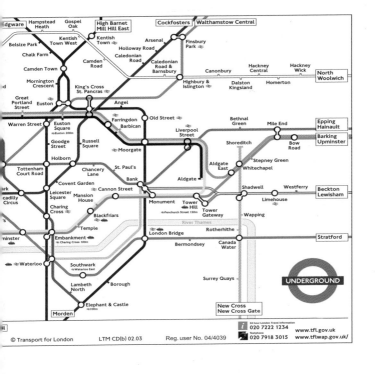

24 hour London Travel Information
020 7222 1234
Textphone
020 7918 3015

www.tfl.gov.uk
www.tflwap.gov.uk/

MAIN SIGHTS

THE CITY★★★

■ St Paul's Cathedral★★★

⊖ *St Paul's.* The present cathedral, the fourth or fifth on a site dating back to AD 604, is considered to be the masterpiece of **Sir Christopher Wren** (1632-1723), though it is worth visiting some of his other churches in the City (eg St Stephen Walbrook, St Margaret Lothbury) to gain a fuller impression of the flexibility and ingenuity of Wren's art. After the Great Fire Old St Paul's was a sad ruin; Wren submitted plans for a new cathedral to the authorities before going ahead as Surveyor General to the King's Works. The foundation stone was laid on 21 June 1675. 33 years later Wren saw his son set the final stone in place – the topmost in the lantern. When Wren died 15 years later he

was buried within the walls; beneath the dome his own epitaph reads in Latin: "Reader, if you seek his monument, look around you."

Exterior – The most striking feature is the **dome**, even today a dominant feature of the City skyline. Unlike the dome of St Peter's, which fascinated and influenced Wren, it is not a true hemisphere. The drum below it is in two tiers, the lower encircled by columns and crowned by a balustrade, the upper recessed behind the balustrade so as to afford a circular viewing gallery, the **Stone Gallery**. On top of the dome, the lantern is restrained English Baroque with columns on all four sides and a small cupola serving as a plinth to the 6.5ft/2m-diameter golden ball. The **west end** is composed of a two-tier portico of Corinthian and composite columns below a decorated pediment surmounted by the figure of Saint Paul. On either side rise Wren's most Baroque spires as a foil to the dome. A notable feature of the exterior is the profuse carving by Gibbons and others.

K. Bratz/MICHELIN

"St Stephen Walbrook"

Interior – The immediate impression is one of space, of almost luminescent stone and, in the distance, gold and mosaic. In the **nave** the entire space between two piers in the north aisle is occupied by the Wellington monument; in the north transept hangs Holman Hunt's *The Light of the World*. From the **Whispering Gallery** in the dome *(259 steps)* there are impressive views of the concourse below, the choir, arches and clerestory, and close views of the interior of the dome, painted by Thornhill. A whisper spoken close to the wall can be clearly heard on the diametrically opposite side. The **views***** from the **Golden Gallery** at the top of the dome are better than from the Stone Gallery *(543 steps)*. The **transepts** are shallow, that to the north serving as baptistery (18C font), that to the south including a fine statue of **Nelson**. In the

choir the dark oak stalls are the exquisite work of **Grinling Gibbons**. The iron railing, the gates to the choir aisles and the great gilded screens enclosing the sanctuary are the work of Jean Tijou. The graceful sculpture of the Virgin and Child in the north aisle is by Henry Moore (1984). In the south aisle is a rare pre-Fire relic, a statue of **John Donne**, the great poet and Dean of St Paul's 1621-31.

Guildhall : Magog

The **Crypt** contains tombs of many illustrious individuals and memorials to the dead of many wars and to others, too numerous to list.

■ Barbican★

⊖ *Barbican.* The project (1962-82) combines residential accommodation with schools, shops, open spaces, a conference and arts centre, a medieval church and the Museum of London. The rounded arch motif, used vertically in the arcades and on the roofline and horizontally round the stairwells, gives a sense of unity to the various elements which are linked by high and low level walkways.

■ Tower of London★★★

⊖ *Tower Hill.* William I constructed a wooden fortress in 1067, replacing it by one in stone (c 1077-97) in order to deter Londoners from revolt; its vantage point beside the river also gave immediate sighting of any hostile force coming up the Thames. Norman, Plantagenet and Tudor successors recognised its value and extended it.

From 1300-1810 the Tower housed the Royal Mint; because of its

High-rise living in the Barbican

defences it became the Royal Jewel House and served as a grim prison.

The **Jewel House** displays the **Crown Jewels★★★** which date from the Restoration to the present day, almost all of the earlier regalia having been sold or melted down by Cromwell. The **Chapel of St Peter ad Vincula**, consecrated in the 12C, rebuilt in the 13C and 16C, is the burial place of several dukes and two of Henry VIII's queens, beheaded in the Tower.

Traitors' Gate was the main entrance to the Tower when the Thames was still London's principal thoroughfare; later, when the river served only as a secret means of access, the entrance acquired its chilling name. The Bloody Tower was perhaps the place where the little Princes in the Tower were murdered in 1483. Sir Walter Ralegh was imprisoned in it from 1603-15.

The keep, known as the **White Tower★★★**, is one of the earliest fortifications on such a scale in western Europe, begun by William I in 1078 and completed 20 years later by William Rufus. The stone walls (100ft/31m high) form an uneven quadrilateral, its corners marked by one circular and three square towers. The **Armour Collection**, one of the world's greatest, was started by Henry VIII and increased under Charles II. On the second floor **St John's Chapel★★** (1080) is a stone chapel (55ft/17m long) rising through two floors. An inner line of great round columns with simply carved capitals bear circular Norman arches which enfold the apse in an ambulatory and are echoed above in a second tier beneath the tunnel vault.

Beauchamp Tower★, built in the 13C, has served as a place of confinement since the 14C. The walls of the main chamber are inscribed with graffiti.

■ Tower Bridge★★

The familiar Gothic towers, high-level walkways (*lift or 200 steps*) and the original engine rooms form part of the tour which traces the design of the bridge by Sir John Wolfe-Barry and Horace Jones, its construction (1886-94) and explains the functioning of the hydraulic mechanism which raised the 1100t bascules, until 1976. Panoramic **views★★★** from the walkways.

■ St Katharine Docks★

In 1828, on the site of the 12C Hospital of St Katharine by the Tower, **Thomas Telford** developed a series of basins and warehouses; the dock was the nearest to the City and prospered for over a hundred years. After wartime bombing the dock was abandoned until 1968, when moorings were organised for private yachts. Telford's Italianate building was restored as Ivory House with apartments above a shopping arcade.

■ HMS Belfast

The cruiser (1938) moored against the south bank of the Thames saw service with the North Atlantic Convoys and on D-Day in 1944.
Nearby is **City Hall**, one of London's latest architectural landmarks overlooki joys superb views of the river, of the Tower of London and of Tower Bridge.

■ Southwark★

⊖ *Southwark*. The Borough of Southwark, also known familiarly as "The Borough", takes its name from the defence at the south end of London Bridge. It became both famous

Hay's Galleria

J. Malburet/MICHELIN

and infamous in the 16C as a location, outside the jurisdiction of the City, for brothels and theatres. Near the site of the original **Globe Theatre**, where Shakespeare's plays were performed, now stands the **International Shakespeare Globe Centre**, constructed with 16C techniques, to promote an appreciation of Shakespeare's plays in an authentic setting. Tate Modern and the Millennium Bridge to St Paul's add to the vitality of the area. The **Bramah Museum of Tea and Coffee** traces the fashion in these beverages. One of the few medieval buildings to survive is the **George Inn★**, built round a courtyard, although only one of the galleried ranges has survived. The old warehouses have been converted to new uses – **Hays Galleria** with its shops, pubs and modern sculpture. The river front boasts the **Design Museum**, which illustrates the

The Lloyd's building

Ph. Gajic/MICHELIN

evolution of contemporary design, and restaurants with a view of the City. Under the arches of London Bridge Station is the **London Dungeon**, a gruesome spectacle of punishment in past centuries. Further along is **Winston Churchill's Britain at War**, a nostalgic reconstruction of life during the blitz.

■ Southwark Cathedral★★

The earliest work is the fragment of a Norman arch in the north wall. The massive piers supporting the central tower and the intimately proportioned Early

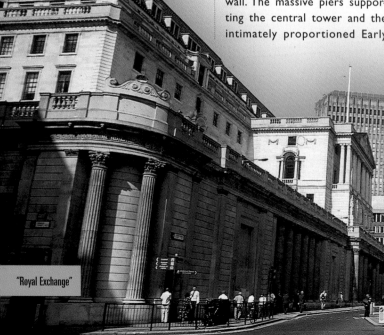

"Royal Exchange"

English **chancel** date from the 13C. The **altar screen** (1520) appears in sumptuous Gothic glory. The nave was rebuilt in 1890-97 to harmonise with the chancel. Notable features are the **Harvard Chapel** (*north chancel aisle*), the 1616 **monument** to Alderman Humble and his wives (*north of altar screen*) and the 12 **bosses** from a 15C wooden roof (*west wall*). The his-tory of the cathedral is traced in the visitor centre where vestiges of earlier structures are visible; the library affords a fine view of the roofline. ■

WESTMINSTER ★★★

■ **Westminster Abbey★★★**
⊖ *Westminster, Victoria.* The abbey, in which William the Conqueror was crowned as **William I** on Christmas Day 1066, was built by **Edward the Confessor** in the Norman style; only after the rebuilding by the Plantagenet Henry III in 1220 did it acquire its Gothic appearance. Inspired by the style of Amiens and Reims, Henry III began with the Lady Chapel, to provide a noble shrine for the Confessor, who had been canonised in 1163. Gradually the existing building was demolished as new replaced the old; progress halted after the construction of the first bay of the nave and it was another two centuries before the

Changing of the Guard

Ph. Gajic/MICHELIN

nave was finished. When Henry VII constructed his **chapel** at the east end (1503-19), Perpendicular Gothic was still the ecclesiastical style and he produced the jewel of the age. The west towers by Wren and Nicholas Hawksmoor (1722-45) and repairs by George Gilbert Scott kept to the Gothic spirit. The Dissolution in 1540 meant the confiscation of the abbey's treasure, forfeiture of its property and the disbanding of the 600-year-old Benedictine community of 50 monks, but not the destruction of the buildings. In 1560 Queen Elizabeth I granted a charter establishing the Collegiate Church of St Peter with a royally appointed Dean and chapter of 12 canons and the College of St Peter, generally known as Westminster School.

Interior – The vaulting is glorious, the carving on screens and arches delicate, often beautiful, sometimes humorous; the ancient tombs in **Henry VII's**, **St Edward's** and the ambulatory chapels are dignified and sometimes revealing in expression (some being derived from death masks). The transepts and aisles abound with sculpted monuments, particularly in the famous **Poets' Corner★** *(south transept)*.

The **Sanctuary** beyond the **Choir** is where the **Coronation ceremony** is performed. To the right hangs a 16C tapestry behind a large 15C altarpiece of rare beauty. Beyond is an ancient 13C sedilia painted with full length royal figures (Henry III, Edward I). The **Henry VII Chapel★★★** with its superb fan-vaulted roof is the most glorious of the abbey's many treasures. The banners of the Knights Grand

Sentry Duty at Horse Guards

Ph. Gajic/MICHELIN

Cross of the **Order of the Bath** hang still and brilliant above the stalls patterned with the heraldic plates of former occupants and those of their esquires, with inventive 16C-18C misericords. The **Chapel of Edward the Confessor**** is rich in history, with the Confessor's shrine ringed with the tombs of five kings and three queens. In the centre against a carved stone **screen** (1441) stands the Coronation Chair which contained the Stone of Scone beneath the seat.

The **Chapter House**** (1248-53) is an octagonal chamber (60ft/18m in diameter) with vaulting springing from a slim central pier of attached Purbeck marble columns. Its walls are partially decorated with medieval paintings.

■ **Buckingham Palace****
⊖ *Green Park, St James's Park*. The house built by the newly-created Duke of Buckingham in 1703 on land granted to him by Queen Anne was purchased in 1762 by George III for his bride Charlotte. Under George IV it was converted into a palace (1825-37) by John Nash and Edward Blore; the east front containing the famous balcony was added in 1847.

The tour includes the Throne Room, the Drawing Rooms, the Ballroom, the Dining Room and the Picture Gallery, hung with Royal portraits and old masters from the Royal Collection and furnished with many pieces collected by George IV.

Changing of the Guard** takes place in the forecourt. When the Sovereign is in residence, the Royal Standard flies over the Palace.

The **Queen's Gallery**** presents exhibitions of the portraits, paintings, drawings and furniture in the superb Royal Collection.

■ Whitehall★★

⊖ *Westminster, Charing Cross.* The wide street, which leads north from Parliament Square and Parliament Street, is lined by government offices. In the middle stands the **Cenotaph**, an austere war memorial. On the left is Downing Street, where a modest Georgian house (n° 10) has been the residence of the Prime Minister since it was rebuilt for Sir Robert Walpole in 1732.

The **Banqueting House★★**, the only part of Whitehall Palace to survive, was designed by Inigo Jones, begun for James I in 1619; the north entrance and staircase were added in 1809 and the exterior refaced in 1829. The hall is a double cube (110 x 55 x 55ft/ 33.5 x 16.75 x 16.75m) with a delicate balcony on gilded corbels; the compartmented ceiling is decorated with magnificent paintings (1634-35) by Rubens. It was on a platform erected in front of this building that Charles I was executed in January 1649.

Opposite stands **Horse Guards★**, an unadorned mid-18C building distinguished by the statue-like **Household Cavalry sentries**. A central arch beneath a clock tower leads to the parade ground, where Trooping the Colour takes place in June, and to St James's Park.

■ St James's Park★★

⊖ *St James's Park.* The oldest royal park in London dates from 1532 when Henry VIII had **St James's Palace** built in place of an old hospital for lepers. The park was landscaped in the 19C by John Nash who was also responsible for the majestic **Carlton House Terrace★** in the northeast corner. From the bridge over the water there is a fine **view** of Whitehall and Buckingham Palace.

■ Palace of Westminster★★★

The palace built by Edward the Confessor was enlarged and embellished by the medieval English kings but most of the surviving buildings, by then occupied by Parliament, were destroyed in a disastrous fire in 1834. The oldest remaining part is **Westminster Hall**★★ which William Rufus added to his father's palace between 1097 and 1099. This scene of royal banquets and jousts in the Middle Ages was altered and re-roofed by command of Richard II between 1394 and 1399. For this the upper parts were rebuilt and what is perhaps the finest timber roof of all time was built, a superb

Philippe GUERSAN / © AISI

"Royal Courts of Justice"

hammerbeam★★★ designed by the king's master carpenter, Hugh Herland, carved with flying angels. After the 1834 fire which, fortunately, did not damage Westminster Hall, **Charles Barry** and **Augustus Pugin** won a competition for a new design for the Palace, which became known as the Houses of Parliament. This masterpiece of Victorian Gothic architecture was completed in 1860, with over 1 000 rooms, 100 staircases and 2mi/3km of corridors spread over 8 acres/3ha.

The Clock Tower (316ft/96m), the most famous feature of this distinctive building, was completed by 1859. The name **Big Ben**★ applied originally to the great bell;

its diameter is 9ft/2.75m, its height 7ft/2.1m and it weighs 13.5t. The light above the clock remains lit while the House of Commons is sitting.

The **House of Commons***, rebuilt after being bombed in 1941, seats 437 of the 659 elected Members of Parliament; at the end of this simply decorated chamber is the canopied Speaker's Chair. Red stripes on both sides of the green carpet mark the limit to which a Member may advance to address the House – the distance between the stripes is reputedly that of two drawn swords.

The **House of Lords**** is a symphony of design and workmanship in encrusted gold and scarlet. The throne and steps, beneath a Go-

thic canopy mounted on a wide screen, all in gold, occupy one end of the chamber. The ceiling is divided by ribs and gold patterning above the red buttoned leather benches and the Woolsack, seat of the Lord Chancellor since the reign of Edward III, adopted as a symbol of the importance to England of the wool trade. ∎

WEST END★

■ Trafalgar Square★★

⊖ *Charing Cross, Westminster*. The square was laid out by Nash in 1820 as part of a north-south route between Bloomsbury and Westminster. Begun in 1829, the square was completed in the 1840s, when Charles Barry levelled it and built the north terrace for the National Gallery. In 1842 **Nelson's Column** was erected; the monument is 185ft/56m tall, with the pedestal, fluted granite column, bronze capital and a statue (17ft/4.5m) of the great admiral who lost his life winning the Battle of Trafalgar. A plan to reclaim the area for pedestrian access and to hold events in the square will give a new impetus to this national landmark, where people congregate in times of strife or celebration.

The 18C church of **St Martin-in-the-Fields★** *(northeast)* has a Corinthian portico and an elegant spire. Note the equestrian statue *(south)* of **Charles I** cast by Le Sueur in 1633 and *(west)* **Canada House**, a classical building of Bath stone (1824-27).

Trafalgar Square

A National Hero

Horatio Nelson, 1st Viscount (1758-1805), was the son of a Norfolk clergyman. He went to sea aged 12 and rose through the ranks to become captain in 1793. During various French revolutionary actions, he lost his right eye (1794) and his right arm (1797) before defeating the French at Aboukir Bay (1798), and destroying their fleet at Trafalgar. It was during this final campaign that he died from a musket wound to the shoulder (the ball is conserved at the National Maritime Museum in Greenwich, as are many letters, personal possessions and memorabilia).

■ Covent Garden★★

⊖ *Covent Garden, Leicester Sq, Charing Cross.* Covent Garden piazza, the first London square, was designed by Inigo Jones in 1631 for the 4th Earl of Bedford who had been granted the land, once the property of Westminster Abbey, by Henry VIII. It was originally surrounded by colonnades, long demolished; **St Paul's Church** however, still stands, its elegant portico dominating the west side of the square.

At the centre are the **Central Market Buildings**, designed in 1832 by Charles Fowler, to house the fruit and vegetable market which moved out in 1974. The tiny shops and market stalls now sell a great variety of goods – books, cooking pots, fashion, jewellery, crafts and refreshment; musicians and street artists perform on the open cobblestones.

Floral Hall,
Royal Opera House

J. Malburet/MICHELIN

Coffee Houses

The fashion for coffee houses was introduced to London during the Commonwealth (1652). Originally they served as meeting places in the City for the exchange of business intelligence. By 1715 there were over 500 not only in the City but also in Covent Garden and the Strand, St James's, Mayfair and Westminster. Customers of like interests would gather regularly, even daily, in the same houses or call at several houses at different times to pick up messages and even letters or to read the news sheets, which at first circulated from one house to another, and the later newspapers (*Daily Courant*, 1702) which were available to customers for the price of a single cup of hot chocolate or coffee. At the end of the 18C the City coffee houses reverted to being pubs and the West End houses disappeared, except **Boodle's** and **White's** which became clubs.

Of the 17C and 18C coffee houses for which Covent Garden was as famous as the City, none remain: **Will's**, frequented by "all the wits in town" according to Pepys used to stand at n° 1 Bow Street, **Button's** in Russell Street, the **Bedford**, the **Piazza**...

The old flower market now houses the **Theatre Museum** and **London's Transport Museum**★. The **Royal Opera House**★ and the Floral Hall have been beautifully refurbished − panoramic **views** from the terrace.

Browsing in Covent Garden Market

Chinatown

■ Soho*

⊖ *Leicester Sq, Piccadilly Circus, Tottenham Court Rd, Oxford Circus.* This very cosmopolitan district, where immigrants tended to congregate, is now the home of the music and film trades, evening entertainment (theatres and restaurants) and night-life (clubs and discos). **Leicester Square*** is a pleasant tree-shaded pedestrian precinct containing the **Half-Price Ticket Booth** and a statue of Charlie Chaplin. The **Trocadero Complex** is composed of the original Trocadero, a 19C music-hall, and the London Pavilion (1885), first a theatre and then a cinema, which have been converted to house shops and restaurants.

A Roll-Call of Luminaries

William Blake was born in Soho (1757), Hazlitt died there (1830); Edmund Burke, Sarah Siddons, Dryden, Sheraton lived there; Marx, Engels, Canaletto, Haydn lodged there; Mendelssohn and Chopin gave recitals at the 18C house in Meard Street of Vincent Novello, father of Ivor and founder of the music publishers. J L Baird first demonstrated television in Frith Street in 1926...

Statue of Charlie Chaplin, Leicester Square

Ritz Hotel

The 130-bedroom hotel was opened on 24 May 1906 by César Ritz, a Swiss waiter turned entrepreneur, at the height of the Edwardian era. It was an immediate success, bordering on the decorous and the decadent with single rooms costing 10s 6d a night (52½p)! Externally, the early frame structure was fashioned by Mewès and Davis to the French Classical style, while inside all was gilded Louis XVI decoration and marble. Regular patrons have included royalty (the future Edward VII, the Duke of Windsor and Wallis Simpson, Queen Elizabeth the Queen Mother), the rich (the late Aga Khan, Aristotle Onassis), the glamorous (Rita Hayworth) and the plain famous (Noel Coward, Charlie Chaplin, Winston Churchill)... During the 1970s and 1980s a selection of spare jackets and ties was supplied so that pop stars might conform with the strict dress code.

■ Piccadilly Circus★

⊖ Piccadilly Circus, Green Park, Hyde Park Corner. This famous road junction, once considered the hub of the British Empire, is still dominated by **Eros**, the Angel of Christian Charity, surmounting the fountain erected in memory of the philanthropist, **Lord Shaftesbury**, in 1892. Shaftesbury Avenue (1886), created as a slum-clearance measure, is now at the heart of theatreland. With its distinctive illuminated hoardings, it is a popular meeting-point for visitors and Londoners alike.

J. Malburet/MICHELIN

Eros, Piccadilly Circus

Shepherd Market: terrases

■ Mayfair★

⊖ *Bond Street, Green Park.* The most luxurious district of London takes its name from a cattle and general fair held annually in May until it was closed in 1706 for unruly behaviour. It contains the most elegant hotels and the greatest concentration of smart shops: **Burlington Arcade★** (1819) where the bow-fronted boutiques sell fashion, jewellery, leather goods; **Bond Street★** famous for art auctioneers and dealers (Sotheby's, Phillips, Agnew's, Colnaghi), jewellery (Asprey, Cartier) and fashion (Fenwick, Yves St Laurent); **Regent Street** well known for elegant stores (Austin Reed, Aquascutum, Burberry, Jaeger and Liberty); **Oxford Street** lined with the more popular department stores (John Lewis, Selfridges and Marks & Spencer).

J. Malburet/MICHELIN

Handel in Mayfair

George Frederick Handel (1685-1759) came to England in 1711 in the wake of George IV; his Italian operas were received with great acclaim. Over a period of 18 years he wrote nearly 30 such operas and, as popularity for this genre waned, he turned to composing oratorios with as much success, setting works by Milton and Congreve – adapted by Pope and Dryden.
Handel lived at 25 Brook Street for 36 years; it was here that he composed *Messiah*. He was a practising Christian and a regular attender at St George's.

Rare view of medieval London —
half-timbered buildings, Staple Inn, Holborn

■ Holborn★

⊖ *Holborn, Chancery Lane*. The medieval manors at this former crossroads have been transformed into Lincoln's Inn and Gray's Inn. The fields where beasts once grazed are less in extent but still open; on the north side stands **Sir John Soane's Museum**★★ which presents an eclectic collection of Classical sculpture, architectural fragments, drawings, prints and paintings (Hogarth, Canaletto).

Lincoln's Inn★★ dates back to the late 15C with its buildings of brick with stone decoration, and inter-communicating courts. The Old Hall dates from 1490, the Old Buildings are Tudor, refaced in 1609, while the Chapel was rebuilt in 1620-23.

Gray's Inn★ dates from the 14C in its foundation, from the 16C in its buildings; many have been renewed since the war. A remarkable survival from the late 16C is the row of **half-timbered houses** (1586-96), forming the front of **Staple Inn**★, as is a little half-timbered house, known as the Old Curiosity Shop *(in Portsmouth Street, southwest of Lincoln's Inn Fields)*, which is said to be one of the oldest in London (c 1500).

■ Bloomsbury★

◯ *Tottenham Court Road. Goodge Street, Russell Square.* The once residential area with its many squares is dominated by two learned institutions, the British Museum and London University. The development of Bloomsbury Square in 1661 brought a new concept in social planning; the 4th Earl of Southampton erected houses for the well-to-do around three sides of a square, a mansion for himself on the fourth, northern side and a network of service streets all around with a market nearby. The elegant **Bedford Square★★** (1775) is still complete, with its three-storey brick terrace houses with rounded doorways and first-floor balconies. Other squares followed in the 19C. The most famous residents of these squares were the **Bloomsbury Group** of writers, artists and philosophers, loosely centred around the figures of Virginia Woolf, Vanessa Bell, Roger Fry and others in the 1920s. ■

London University

London University moved from Piccadilly to Bloomsbury after the Second World War, although construction of the **Senate House**, a cold Portland stone building with a tall square tower (library) by Charles Holden, began in 1932. Colleges, faculties and new institutes are now housed throughout the immediate neighbourhood in old 18C-19C houses and in the ever-extending, heterogeneous complex of brick, stone, concrete, steel, mosaic and glass.

Bedford Square

KENSINGTON ★★

■ Kensington Palace★★

⊖ *High Street Kensington, South Kensington, Notting Hill Gate, Holland Park.* Since its purchase in 1689 by William III this early-17C Jacobean house has passed through three phases: under the House of Orange it was the monarch's private residence, with **Wren** as principal architect; under the early Hanoverians it became a royal palace; since 1760 it has been a residence for members of the royal fasmily.

The **State Apartments** are approached by the Queen's Staircase designed by Wren. The **Queen's Gallery** has carving by Grinling Gibbons and portraits by Kneller and Lely. The **Privy** and lofty **Presence Chamber**, **Cupola** and **Drawing Rooms**, added for George I in 1718-20, were decorated by William Kent from 1722 to 1727. The staircase, built by Wren in 1689, was altered in 1692-93 and again when Kent covered the walls and ceiling with *trompe-l'oeil* paintings including a dome and gallery of contemporary courtiers. The gallery was built to house William's finest pictures. Kent's ceiling depicts scenes from the story of Ulysses.

The Court Dress Collection displayed in period room settings *(ground floor)* shows the dresses and uniforms worn at the select court occasions spanning 12 reigns from 1750.

Royal Ceremony

The **Court Dress Collection** traces the evolution of court dress from the 18C to the 20C. Dictated by protocol, elegant dresses and accessories (Orders of Chivalry), court suits and ceremonial uniforms resplendent with gold and silver, lace and embroidery, worn at levées and at court are presented in contemporary settings. More contemporary exhibits include pieces from the Queen's wardrobe, largely designed by the late Sir Norman Hartnell to suit the sovereign's various State functions.

■ Kensington Gardens★★

The gardens (originally 26 acres/10ha and extended finally to 275 acres/110ha) were at their prime under the Queens Mary, Anne and Caroline (George II's consort) and the royal gardeners, Henry Wise and his successor, Charles Bridgeman. In the 18C the **Round Pond** was dug, facing the State Apartments, as the focal point for avenues radiating to the **Serpentine** and **Long Water**, which terminates in the 19C Italian Gardens and Queen Anne's Alcove. Other features of the period are the **Broad Walk** and the early-18C **Orangery★**, a splendidly Baroque centrepiece.

Beyond the Flower Walk (south) stands the **Albert Memorial★**

P. Guensan ©AGSI

(1876), designed by George Gilbert Scott. The neo-Gothic spire is ornamented with mosaics, pinnacles and a cross. At the centre, surrounded by allegorical statues and a frieze of poets, artists, architects and composers, sits a gilded bronze statue (14ft/4.25m) of the Prince Consort.

Opposite stands the **Royal Albert Hall** (1867-71), a popular venue for meetings, conferences and concerts, notably the **Promenade Concerts**. Note the decorative frieze with graceful symbols of the Arts and Sciences. A dignified statue of Prince Albert dominates the formal south entrance.

"Feeding the ducks"

Further south are the Science Museum, The Natural History Museum and the Victoria and Albert Museum, all part of the great educational centre established by Prince Albert with the profits from the Great Exhibition held in 1851 in Hyde Park. To house the Great Exhibition, Joseph Paxton designed the **Crystal Palace** (19 acres/ 7.5ha), a metal and glass structure, which was re-erected at Sydenham but destroyed by fire in 1936.

■ Hyde Park★★

⊖ *Marble Arch, Hyde Park Corner, Lancaster Gate, Queensway, Bayswater.* This less formal park extends east of the Serpentine to Park Lane. Pitt the Elder called it and Kensington Gardens "the lungs of London"; 250 years later the park still enables residents, office-workers and tourists to

Royal Albert Hall

J. Malburet/MICHELIN

enjoy the fresh air with bandstands for summer music, boating on the Serpentine, riding along Rotten Row, bowling and putting greens and tennis courts.

Speakers' Corner is a relatively modern feature of the park; not until 1872 did the government recognise the need for a place of public assembly and free discussion. To its north stands **Marble Arch**, designed by John Nash in 1827 as a grand entrance to Buckingham Palace, in commemoration of the battles of Trafalgar and Waterloo. ■

Michelin House in Art Nouveau style

K. Brett/MICHELIN

51

CHELSEA ★★

Although the completion of the Embankment in 1874 removed the atmosphere of a riverside community evoked in paintings by Rowlandson, Turner and Whistler, Chelsea continued to attract artists, architects, writers, actors and gained a reputation for Bohemian living.

In 1537 Henry VIII built a riverside palace on a site now occupied by 19-26 Cheyne Walk. His chancellor, Sir Thomas More, had built a large house near the river where he lived from 1523 until his execution in 1535. A seated figure of More is outside **Chelsea Old Church** which dates from pre-Norman times. It has a 13C chancel but, after bomb damage, the tower and nave were rebuilt in their original style of 1670.

Chelsea Luminaries

A varied group of notable people has lived in Chelsea: the famous actresses Nell Gwynne, Dame Ellen Terry, Dame Sybil Thorndyke (who inspired GB Shaw to write *St Joan* for her); Sir Joseph Banks (botanist, explorer and President of the Royal Society); Sir John Fielding (a respected magistrate who was blind from birth), the engineers **Sir Marc Isambard Brunel** and his son Isambard Kingdom; Charles Kingsley (author of *The Water Babies*); Mrs Elizabeth Gaskell (novelist); the **Pre-Raphaelite** poets and painters **Dante Gabriel Rossetti**, his sister Christina, Burne-Jones, William and Jane Morris, Holman Hunt, Swinburne, Millais. Other artists include **William de Morgan**, Wilson Steer, Sargent, Augustus John, Orpen, Sickert. Mark Twain, **Henry James**, TS Eliot are among Chelsea Americans. Smollett lived in Lawrence Street, **Oscar Wilde** at 34 Tite Street, AA Milne at 13 Mallord Street (1919-42). There were also Hilaire Belloc, the Sitwells, Arnold Bennett...

■ King's Road

This used to be the route taken by Charles II when calling upon Nell Gwynne at her house in Fulham: between 1719 and 1830, the King's Road was closed to all but those holding a royal pass owing to its attraction to footpads. It is now famous for its shops selling fashion accessories and antiques, restaurants and pubs, while the small streets around are lined by traditional cottages once built for artisans.

■ Cheyne Walk★

The terraces of brick houses standing back from the river front are rich with memories of artists, writers and royalty. Corinthian pilasters and an entablature mark the entrance to n° 4 where the painter Daniel Maclise lived and George Eliot spent her last weeks. Beautiful railings and fine urns distinguish n° 5; n° 6 is remarkable for the Chinese-Chippendale gate and railings.

VERSE FROM A POPULAR SONG

"Though the philistines might jostle, you would rank as an apostle

In the high aesthetic band

If you swanned down Cheyne Walk with just a sunflower on a stalk

In your medieval hand."

■ Royal Hospital★★

⊖ *Sloane Sq.* The hospital was founded by King Charles II in 1682 as a retreat for veterans of the regular army. It was undoubtedly inspired by the Hôtel des Invalides in Paris, founded by Louis XIV in 1670.

Wren produced a quadrangular plan with a main court open to the south towards the river and the grounds, in which the **Chelsea Flower Show** is held every summer; he expanded it by abutting courts to east and west, always leaving one side open. The main entrance is beneath the lantern-crowned octagon porch in the north range of the original **Figure Court**, named after the classical statue of Charles II by **Grinling Gibbons** at the centre. From the octagon porch, steps rise to the **Chapel** (barrel vault, plasterwork, domed apse) and **Great Hall** (18C mural of Charles II in front of the hospital), both panelled beneath tall rounded windows.

J. Malburet/MICHELIN

The "Old Soldiers" themselves can be seen in their blue un-dress or even scarlet full-dress uniforms, out and about on the nearby streets.

Houseboats

Moored on the river are several permanent houseboats: larger and more spacious than a canal barge, these would once have accommodated watermen and river pilots. Today they provide homes for a more Bohemian set of Chelsea residents.

■ Carlyle's House

24 Cheyne Row – ⊖ *Sloane Sq.* The modest Queen Anne house was the home (1834-81) of the historian Thomas Carlyle; it contains portraits, personal relics, books and furniture. ■

Royal Hospital, Chelsea

MUSEUMS AND GALLERIES

■ British Museum★★★

Bloomsbury – ⊖ *Tottenham Court Road, Russell Square.* When Sir Hans Sloane's collection was bequeathed to the nation in 1753 Parliament was encouraged to found the British Museum.

Already in the vaults in Westminster lay Sir Robert Cotton's (1570-1631) priceless collection of medieval manuscripts and the old Royal Library of 12 000 volumes assembled by monarchs since Tudor times. As more and more collections were presented a separate building became necessary. Montagu House was bought with money raised in a lottery and the Museum opened in 1759. Exhibits were displayed unlabelled, causing Cobbett to call the museum "the old curiosity shop".

To house the burgeoning collection Smirke produced plans which culminated in the replacement of Montagu House by the present building and its later additions. The early sequence of acquisitions, increased in the 19C and 20C by finds by archaeologists attached to the museum, brought the Museum its reputation as one of the greatest centres of world antiquities. Notable among the Egyptian antiquities are the **mummies** and the **Rosetta Stone**. The collection of Western Asiatic antiquities is particularly wide-ranging, while the Greek and Roman antiquities include the **Elgin Marbles** (sculptures from the Parthenon) and the exquisite Roman **Portland Vase**. The Oriental collection with its fine T'ang horses is no less significant. In the Prehistoric and Romano-British and Medieval sections admire the craftsmanship of the shields, helmets and delicate golden torcs. **Lindow Man** (1C AD) is evidence of ritual practices. Reminders of

© The British Museum

Portland Vase

Roman Britain are the 4C silver set of tableware, the **Mildenhall Treasure**, and **Royal Gold Cup**. The mid-12C **Lewis Chessmen** are Scandinavian in origin and the **Sutton Hoo Ship Burial** reveals the rich trappings of an Anglo-Saxon royal tomb.

Old British Library – In 1973, the British Museum's library departments were vested in a separate authority and granted funds to have new premises built in St Pancras. The circular, domed **Reading Room** (40ft/12m wide), which dates from 1857 and was designed to ensure that the "poorest student" as well as men of letters should be able to have access to the library, has been a haven of learning for scholars and famous men. It is now a high-tech information centre used for research and a new public reference library. The Grand Rooms are being restored to their former glorious Regency decorative schemes; the King's Library will provide displays relating to the Age of Enlightenment and connoisseurship; Classical sculpture will be displayed in the Manuscripts Saloon. The North Library will provide an introduction to the Ethnography Collections.

■ **British Library**
Euston Road – ⊖ *King's Cross-St Pancras*. The British Library was designed by Professor Sir Colin St John Wilson and is a free-form, asymmetric building of red

New light on the Classical splendour of the Great Court

brick, Welsh slate roofs, metal and granite weatherings. The entrance piazza is dominated by a monumental bronze statue of Newton (after Blake) by Sir Eduardo Paolozzi and by *Planets* by Antony Gormley, a circle of 8 glacial boulders, carved with the contours of a body, resting on pillars. The Library boasts automated systems for the catalogue, requests and book-handling.

The King George III Library is displayed as a backdrop to the entrance hall. The Library's most famous treasures (Magna Carta, Lindisfarne Gospels, the Gutenberg Bible, Diamond Sutra, the Beatles Manuscripts) are on view in the John Ritblat Gallery. The Pearson Gallery of Living Words, organised in five themes, reflects the diversity of the Library's collection through books, manuscripts, interactive displays

Changes for the Third Millennium

The British Museum is undergoing large-scale reorganisation: the **British Library** has moved into new purpose-built premises and the ethnographic collections from the **Museum of Mankind** *(closed to the public)* have been reintegrated into the British Museum.

The **Great Court Project**, by Sir Norman Foster, which entailed the clearance of subsidiary buildings, includes elliptical mezzanine floors for a sophisticated Centre for Education comprising activity areas for young visitors and conference facilities for researchers and academics, the Museum bookshop, temporary thematic exhibition areas and restaurants. The public areas display sculpture which gives a foretaste of the museum's riches.

etc. The Workshop of Words, Sound and Images is a hands-on gallery tracing the story of book production from the earliest written documents to the 20C digital revolution (interactive displays, demonstrations).

■ National Gallery★★★

Trafalgar Square – ⊖ Charing Cross.
After more than a century of discussion the collection was founded by Parliamentary purchase in 1824, its nucleus being 38 pictures collected by City merchant and banker **John Julius Angerstein** (1735-1823). Only in 1838 was the new gallery completed, its pedimented portico of Corinthian columns forming a climax to Trafalgar Square. The architectural style of the Sainsbury Wing (1991), complements the original building.

There are now more than 2 000 paintings in the collection; they represent the jewels in the public domain

Marriage A-la-Mode:
The Marriage Settlement by William Hogarth

from Early to High Renaissance Italian painting, early Netherlandish, German, Flemish, Dutch, French and Spanish pictures and masterpieces of the English 18C. (The fuller representation of British art, particularly the more modern and 20C work of all schools is in Tate Britain and Tate Modern.)

To give an impression of the richness of the collection let the following names, just some of the bright stars in a brilliant constellation, speak for themselves: Duccio, Giotto, Uccello, Fra Angelico, Piero della Francesca, Botticelli, Leonardo da Vinci, Michelangelo, Raphael, Titian, Tintoretto, Veronese, Bellini, Caravaggio, Canaletto and Guardi among the Italians. From the Low Countries Frans Hals, Jan Steen, Vermeer, Rembrandt, de Hooch, Avercamp, Cuyp, Van Dyck and Rubens. Earlier German and Netherlandish work is represented by Dürer, Cranach, Holbein, van der Weyden, Bosch and Memlinc. Hogarth, Reynolds, Gainsborough, Constable, Turner and Lawrence figure among British artists of the 17C-18C. Spanish artists are represented by Velazquez, El Greco and Goya, and French and other European painting after 1800 by artists such as Manet, Degas, Cézanne, Monet, Renoir, Van Gogh, Seurat, Klimt and Friedrich.

■ **Science Museum**★★★

South Kensington – ↔ *South Kensington.* In this factory-laboratory of Man's continuing invention which extends over 7 acres/ nearly 3ha, there are innumerable working models, handles to pull, buttons to push as well as a hands-on experience area, the Launch Pad and Pattern Pod, and an IMAX cinema. In the Wellcome Wing the innovative presentation of the latest advances of science, medicine and technology aims to entertain and stimulate the imagination.

■ **Tate Britain**★★★

Millbank – ↔ *Pimlico, Vauxhall, Westminster.* The gallery developed because within 50 years

of the founding of the National Gallery in 1824 the nation had acquired a large number of pictures – notably through the Turner bequest (1856), the Chantrey bequest for the purchase of works by living artists as well as early masters and through two major collections.

In 1891, Henry Tate, sugar broker and collector of modern art, offered his collection to the nation and £80 000 for a building. The site of the former Millbank prison was offered and in 1897 the Tate opened as the Gallery of Modern British Art. Extensions were added and the collections were enriched by major bequests and endowments by generous patrons. In 1955 the Tate became legally independent of the National Gallery.

After the opening of Tate Modern in 2000, a new focus has been defined for Tate Britain and the site has been upgraded as part of the Centenary Development scheme which provides for more display space and better access and facilities.

The museum is devoted exclusively to **British art from 1500 to the present day** and includes works by British-born artists, by artists from abroad working in Britain or with themes related to Britain. The re-display of the extensive collections focuses on artistic achievement in Britain and illustrates the quality, diversity, character, originality and influence of British art over five centuries. Various themes are explored including Courtly Portraiture, Caricature and Satire in the 18C, the relations between Britain and Italy in the 18C, the making of British History, Landscape and Empire, British artists and the Near East, Art and Victorian Society, War and Memory, Modern Utopias. There are special displays featuring major figures such as Hogarth, Blake, Constable, Bacon, Gilbert and George, Cornelia Parker. The **Clore Gallery** exhibits the works of Turner. New acquisitions are also on view and major exhibitions proclaim the Tate's commitment to promote British art.

■ People and Culture

Variety and cosmopolitanism are London's greatest assets. Even in central London, widely differing areas, with contrasting characteristics and histories, lie cheek by jowl as buildings from more than three centuries jostle for space. London's cosmopolitanism derives from its willingness, over many centuries, to embrace and adopt newcomers. There are, of course, many Londoners whose families have belonged to the capital for generations, but the city's enormous population ex-

plosions, in the 16C and 17C, and again, in the 19C and 20C, brought countless people into the city. Most came to find work. Since the 12C, London has been England's (and, later, Britain's) premier city. As such, it was the centre of court and government, of administration, and of trade and finance; all these functions demanded a huge workforce, and continue to do so.

Indeed, the life of the capital itself – its transport, shops, restaurants, schools and all the myriad services upon which Londoners and visitors alike depend – provides a multitude of jobs.

Over the centuries people have come from the English countryside, Scotland, Wales and Ireland, especially when those countries were experiencing poverty and starvation. They came from Europe, among them Huguenots from France in the late 17C, Jews from

J. Malburet/MICHELIN

Eastern Europe and Russia in the late 19C, and refugees from Nazi terror in the 1930s. During the Second World War, London became home to people from all parts of Europe. Since then, partly as a consequence of Britain's past imperial might, people have arrived from Asia, Africa, the Caribbean and the Far East.

All these people, whether they are first generation or multi-generation Londoners, contribute to the city's cosmopolitan flavour. Their personal, social, religious and cultural experiences enrich the city, and in turn they absorb some of the essence of the city and become Londoners themselves.

■ **Victoria and Albert Museum**★★★

South Kensington – ⊖ *South Kensington.* This fabulously rich and varied collection was started, in part, with the purchase of contemporary works manufactured for the Exhibition. It includes the national collection of furniture, British sculpture, textiles, ceramics, silver and watercolours, as well as world-famous displays of fashionable dress, jewellery, Italian Renaissance sculpture, and art from India and the Far East. Since 1909 the Museum has been housed in Aston Webb's idiosyncratic building of brick, terracotta and stone, fittingly adorned with a figure of Prince Albert.

"The imposing mass of Tate Modern"

■ Wallace Collection★★★

Hertford House, Manchester Square – ⊖ *Bond Street, Baker St.* The gathering of one of the world's finer collections of 18C French art was the life's work of the 4th Marquess of Hertford (1800-70) who lived mostly in Paris at his small château, Bagatelle, in the Bois de Boulogne. He greatly increased the family collection of Italian masters, 17C Dutch painting, 18C French furniture and Sèvres porcelain and bought extensively the 18C French painters **Watteau, Boucher** and **Fragonard**. His son Richard Wallace (1818-90), founder and benefactor of the Hertford British Hospital in Paris, having added yet more to the collection, finally brought it to England, where his widow subsequently left it to the nation in 1900. A glass-roofed Sculpture Court, galleries exhibiting the reserve collection and better facilities further enhance the appeal of this charming museum.

■ National Maritime Museum★★

Greenwich. After extensive redevelopment, the museum boasts an impressive single-span glazed roof, the largest in Europe, above a neo-Classical courtyard. It is organised by theme, covering past, present and future aspects in most cases: **Explorers** begins with the stories of Columbus and Cook through to modern sailors and underwater exploration; **Passengers** relates historic stories of migration and also looks at futuristic cruise liners and nautical fashion; **Traders** examines the development of the global economy through maritime trade; **Planet Ocean** focuses on environmental change, biodiversity and sustainable development; **Maritime London** illustrates its impact on Britain's economic and social development; **Trade and Empire** studies the political influences of the travellers. **Sea Power** charts world conflicts through the cen-

A magnificent 18C French cabinet by AC Boule

64

turies and **Nelson** traces the eventful life of this heroic figure. The museum's fine collections of art are on display *(in rotation)* in a new **Art and the Sea** gallery. For children, the new **Bridge** links with the popular **All Hands** gallery.

■ Museum of London★★

London Wall, The City – ⊖ *Barbican, St Paul's.* In an interesting modern building the museum presents the story of London from prehistory to the present day. It is undergoing extensive redevelopment to create a new entrance and additional galleries. It is planned to redisplay the permanent exhibits which include archaeological finds such as sculptures from the Roman temple of Mithras, medieval pilgrim badges, the Cheapside Hoard of Jacobean jewellery; a diorama of the Great Fire, the doors from Newgate Gaol, 19C shops and interiors, the Lord Mayor's Coach, souvenirs of the women's suffrage movement... The development of domestic life and public utility services are illustrated as well as political and fashionable London. **London before London** examines the early inhabitants and their settlements, and the River Thames as a vital link. The **World City** galleries cover the period from 1789 to 1914.

■ Natural History Museum★★

South Kensington – ⊖ *South Kensington, Gloucester Road.* Alfred Waterhouse's vast symmetrical palace, inspired by medieval Rhineland architecture, was opened in 1881 to house the British Museum's ever-growing natural history collection, which today illustrates all forms of life, from the smallest bacteria to the largest creatures, fossils and dinosaurs, minerals and rocks as well as an exhibition of Man's place in evolution. The fascinating history of the planet ranges from natural phenomena to the sustainable use of natural resources.

The high-tech design of the Darwin Centre features an inflatable 'caterpillar' roof and a solar wall with huge stainless steel spider-shaped brackets creating ideal

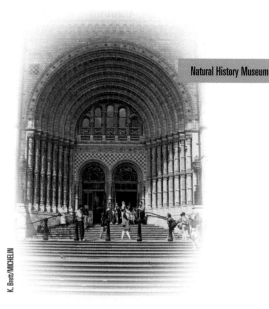

K. Brett/MICHELIN

ambient conditions. The centre aims to make the amazing diversity of its reserve collections as well as the fascinating research carried out by scientists more accessible to the public.

■ Courtauld Institute Galleries★★

Somerset House, The Strand – ⊖ *Charing Cross, Temple, Covent Garden, Holborn.* Since 1990 the Courtauld Institute Galleries have been housed above the gateway in the Strand Block of Somerset House; the **Fine Rooms**, which are notable for their proportions and handsome plaster ceilings, originally housed three learned societies

– the Royal Society, the Antiquaries and the Royal Academy. Somerset House, which was built from 1776-86 of Portland stone, was designed by **Sir William Chambers** as a square of terraced houses overlooking a central courtyard; the south front is supported on a row of massive arches which in the 18C were at the river's edge.

The galleries' collection consists of major art bequests to London University: Samuel Courtauld's private collection of **Impressionists**, including canvases by Manet *(Bar at the Folies-Bergère)*, Degas, Bonnard, Gauguin (Tahitian scenes), Van Gogh *(Self-Portrait with Bandaged Ear)*, Cézanne *(Lake at Annecy)* and Seurat; the Princes Gate Collection comprising 30 oils by **Rubens** and six drawings by **Michelangelo** as well as works by Breugel, Leonardo, Tiepolo, Dürer, Rembrandt, Bellini, Tintoretto and Kokoschka; paintings of the Italian Primitive school and of the Renaissance to the 18C (Gambier Parry and Lee of Fareham collections); and paintings by the **Bloomsbury Group** (Roger Fry donation).

Recently, the displays have been further enriched by glorious 19C-20C works of art from private collections on long-term loan – paintings by artists of the Fauve (Matisse, Derain, Dufy) the Blue Rider (Macke, Pechstein) and other movements (Léger, Delaunay, Van Jawlensky, Kandinsky); and sculpture by major contemporary figures (Degas, Rodin, Laurens, Moore, Hepworth).

■ National Portrait Gallery★★

Trafalgar Square – ⊖ *Leicester Sq, Charing Cross.* The near neighbour of the National Gallery contains portraits of almost every British man or woman of note from the Middle Ages to the present day, some painted, sculpted or photographed by the famous artists of the day. The redisplay of the Tudor Gallery, the Balcony Gallery presenting distinguished contemporary figures, the IT Gallery, state-of-the-art facilities and a restaurant with panoramic **views** have given a dynamic outlook to the gallery.

■ Gilbert Collection★★

Somerset House, The Strand – ⊖ *Charing Cross, Temple, Covent Garden, Holborn.* A glittering array of gold and silver plate, gold boxes, Italian mosaics and

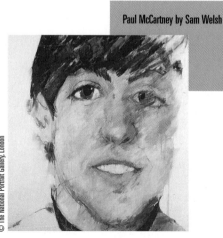

Paul McCartney by Sam Welsh

© The National Portrait Gallery, London

portrait miniatures reflecting the interests of a discerning collector is exhibited in the splendid vaulted rooms in the South and Embankment Buildings with fine **views★★** over the Thames. An 18C barge in the King's Barge House recalls a past era when the Thames was a busy waterway.

The **Hermitage Rooms** *(Somerset House)* which present rotating exhibitions from the prestigious State Hermitage Museum in St Petersburg offer a unique insight into Russian art and history.

■ Imperial War Museum★

Lambeth – ⊖ *Lambeth North, Waterloo, Southwark, Elephant and Castle.* The museum, founded in 1917, was transferred in 1936 to the present building, formerly the

Bethlem Royal Hospital ("Bedlam"), which was designed in 1812-15, with its dome and giant portico added in 1846 by Sydney Smirke.

The museum in no sense glorifies war, but honours those who served. A wide range of weapons and equipment is on display: armoured fighting vehicles, field guns and small arms, together with models, decorations, uniforms, posters and photographs, as well as a selection from the museum's outstanding collection based on the work of two generations of Official War Artists. The **Holocaust Exhibition** is a sober testimony to this sombre page of history.

■ National Army Museum★

Chelsea – ⊖ *Sloane Sq.* The display tells the stirring story of the British Army from the formation of the Yeomen of the Guard by Henry VII on Bosworth Field in 1485 to the present day, in particular the Battle of Waterloo (1815) and the "Forgotten Army" (1939-45). Displays trace the evolution from armour via red coats to battledress and from pikes and swords to revolvers and machine guns. ■

Imperial War Museum

THE ROYAL PARKS

Central London's five main parks were all originally royal possessions, used for hunting as well as for more leisurely pursuits. They form a great green swathe across the centre of the city – crucial breathing-space for local residents, office workers and visitors alike.

■ St James' Park★★
(Tube: St James' Park)
Attractive lake with fountains, magnificent flower beds, bandstand.

■ Green Park
(Tube: Green Park, Hyde Park Corner)
The least varied park – but none-the-less a pleasant swathe of grass and trees. Tradition has it that the area was once a burial-ground for lepers, which is why flowers do not grow well, though there are lovely daffodils in spring.

■ Hyde Park★★
(Tube: Hyde Park Corner, Knightsbridge, Marble Arch, Lancaster Gate)
The Serpentine, a lake formed in 1730 by damming a river,

is the main feature, with boating and swimming in the Lido. There are good views from the bridge. Speaker's Corner and Marble Arch are at the north-east corner.

■ Kensington Gardens★★
(Tube: High Street Kensington, Queensway)

Adjacent to Hyde Park, this is traditionally the most refined of London's parks, with nannies overseeing their charges. The main points of interest are the statue of Peter Pan (by Long Water, a continuation of the Serpentine), the Albert Memorial★, the Flower Walk and the Round Pond. Kensington Palace stands at the western edge.

■ Regent's Park★★★
(Tube: Regent's Park, Baker Street, Camden Town)

The most varied of the parks. John Nash built eight villas in the park and handsome terraces on the east and west sides. On the southern side is Queen Mary's Garden and the Open-Air Theatre, where Shakespearean (and other) productions are staged in summer. On the north side is London Zoo★, created in 1828. It has long been a favourite destination for families and visitors to London. The zoo also incorporates a major research centre. Beyond it is Regent's Canal, with a pleasant towpath walk from Little Venice to Camden Lock. ■

LONDON'S MARKETS

It is not only tourists who head for the capital's numerous markets – but locals as well, so these are some of the best places to get a feel for contemporary life in the capital.

Just looking can be as much fun as buying. If you do feel the need to rest your legs, stop at one of the food stalls or market cafés, where you can usually find ethnic food or perhaps some old-fashioned traditional London fare, such as pie and mash or jellied eels.

Market prices generally are lower than shop prices, and there are plenty of real bargains around. Bear in mind, however, that 'you get what you pay for'. And remember that, unlike shops, stallholders probably will not refund or exchange goods.

Bermondsey: Frequented by professional dealers as well as the public. Paintings, jewellery, silverware, Victoriana etc. *Friday 5am-1pm.*

Berwick Street: Fruit, vegetables and cheese stalls in one of Soho's streets. Rupert Street also has clothes and leather goods, but higher prices. *Daily except Sunday, 9am-5pm.*

Brick Lane: Absolutely everything (or almost), from bicycles to jackets, antiques to electrical goods. Cosier than when it was the haunt of 'Jack the Ripper'. *Sunday 6am-1pm.*

Brixton: A lively food, clothes and general market with a strong Caribbean flavour. Good shops in Granville and Market Row Arcades. *Daily 8.30am-5.30pm except Wednesday pm and Sunday.*

Camden: Five huge, very crowded markets, popular with young people and tourists. The emphasis is on clothes, shoes and jewellery, but there are also books, antiques and crafts. Camden Lock, *Tuesday to Sunday, 10am-6pm*; Camden Market, *Thursday to Sunday, 9am-5.30pm*; other markets at weekends.

Camden Passage: A rather sedate market in Islington (not to be confused with Camden markets), selling prints, silverware, toys, jewellery. Attractive but pricey permanent antique shops. *Wednesday 7am-2pm; Saturday 8am-4pm; Thursday (books) 7am-4pm.*

Columbia Road: One of London's principal retail flower and plant markets (though the flowers are 'left-overs') with interesting shops alongside. *Sunday 8am-12.30pm.*

Greenwich: Antiques, crafts, clothes, books, coins, bric-a-brac. The stalls in the covered market are more expensive. *Saturday and Sunday, 9am-5pm.*

Petticoat Lane: Cheap new goods, such as clothes, jewellery, watches, bags and plenty of raucous backchat. *Sunday 9am-2pm.*

Piccadilly Crafts: Attractive antique and crafts in the churchyard of St James's Piccadilly. *Thursday to Saturday 9.30am-6pm.*

Portobello Road: Thousands of stalls selling paintings, jewellery, silverware, furniture and brick-a-brac. Further on are clothes and craft stalls. Antiques *Saturday 8.30am-5.30pm;* Clothes (under Westway) *Friday 7am-4pm, Saturday 8am-5pm, Sunday 9am-4pm.*

Spitalfields: Craft, bric-a-brac and organic food stalls in the former wholesale market. Organic *Monday to Friday 9am-6pm, Sunday 11am-3pm.* ∎

EXCURSIONS

THE THAMES

The cruise passes a number of famous landmarks, old and new. Opposite Westminster Pier stands **County Hall*** (1922) dominated by the **British Airways London Eye** which affords ex-

In fine weather it is pleasant to take a river cruise downstream from Westminster, Charing Cross or Tower Pier, returning by the foot tunnel under the Thames to Island Gardens, Docklands Light Railway and the underground, or by train to Charing Cross Station or London Bridge Station.

"Cruising down the Thames"

ceptional **views***** to the outer suburbs on a fine day. Just beyond the reconstructed Hungerford Bridge is the **Royal Festival Hall*** (1951), the earliest of the **South Bank Arts Centre**** buildings; later additions are the **Queen Elizabeth Hall** and the **Purcell Room** (1967), the **Hayward Gallery** (1968) – the whole area is scheduled for refurbishment – and the **National Theatre*** (1976) comprising three theatres.

Opposite is the river façade of **Somerset House**** designed by Sir William Chambers in 1777. Further along the Victoria Embankment are *HMS Wellington*, a Second World War frigate converted into the floating hall of the guild of Master Mariners, and *HMS Chrysanthemum*, backed by the gardens of the Inner Temple.

Past Blackfriars Bridge rises the imposing **Tate Modern**** with the elegant Millennium Bridge leading to the north bank. The Globe Theatre, a thatched circular structure, is a distinctive feature.

© Visit London

Beyond Southwark Bridge and Cannon Street Bridge is the *Golden Hinde*, a replica of Sir Francis Drake's galleon, moored near to **Southwark Cathedral★★**. London Bridge (1973) is the latest structure; its predecessor was sold for £1 000 000 and is now in Arizona. Above **Tower Bridge★★** is the **Tower of London★★★** facing *HMS Belfast* (1938) a Second World War cruiser (11 500t), moored beside **Hays Galleria**.

The amazing outline of **City Hall** is a symbol of modernity.

Below the bridge are **St Katharine Docks★** on the north bank and Butler's Wharf, New Concordia and China Wharves (south bank), imaginative developments in the docklands regeneration scheme. The river loops north round the old Surrey Docks *(south bank)* and then south opposite the **Canary Wharf Tower** (1992) on the Isle of Dogs *(north bank)*

Ph. Gajic/MICHELIN

The Playground of London

During the 16C hostelries, brothels (hence the existence of Love Lane), bear-baiting, cock-fighting and other such entertainments were set up in the area stretching westwards between the Liberty of the Clink situated by the **Clink Prison** and **Paris Garden**, named after Robert de Paris, a 14C nobleman.

In the 16C, permission was accorded by the authorities for two theatres to be set up in the old monastery cloisters north of the river in Blackfriars and the area became known as the playground of London.

The reign of the **Rose** (1587), the **Swan** (1595/6), the **Globe** (1599) and the **Hope** (1613) theatres was, however, brief: those that had not already reverted or become bull and bear baiting rings were closed finally under the Commonwealth by the Puritans in 1642.

For entertainment there were the midsummer Southwark Fair, the occasional **frost fairs** when the Thames froze over, the Elizabethan theatres, the brothels and taverns. Not all inns were licentious; many prospered as staging posts for the coaches going south and to the ports and as hostelries for travellers awaiting the morning opening of the bridge to enter the City.

before passing Deptford Creek (*south bank*). The noble buildings of the Old Royal Naval College along the riverside, the Palladian Queen's House and the National Maritime Museum are the pride of Greenwich. The Millennium Dome, a futuristic tented structure, built to mark the advent of the third millennium, stands on the Greenwich peninsula downstream.

■ Tate Modern★★

The former **Bankside Power Station**, a massive structure (1957-60), known to some as the "cathedral of the age of electricity" with its single chimney (325ft/99m) and Aztec-inspired stepped brickwork, was designed by Giles Gilbert Scott. The oil-fired power station which closed in 1981 has been imaginatively converted with the addition of a glass superstructure and large bay windows to house the Tate Gallery's collections of international **20C art**. The wealth of the Tate Modern Art Collection is largely due to the bequests made by Sir Roland Penrose, the one-time friend of Picasso and Ernst, and that of Edward James, a patron of Dali and Magritte. Works by 20C British artists are also on view at Tate Britain.

Gigantic sculptures by contemporary artists are set off by the vast spaces of the dramatic turbine hall (500ft/155m long and 115ft/35m high) where overhead cranes recall the building's industrial past; the amazing perspectives can best be appreciated from the upper galleries. The radical decision to stage themed displays aims to trace the

"View of the Thames from the South Bank"

evolution of genres through the 20C to the present day, to explore various aspects of certain works and to place British art in the international context: Landscape, Matter, Environment; Still Life, Object Real Life; Nude Action and Body; History, Memory, Society. Parallels are drawn between works of different periods, historical and stylistic associations are highlighted to challenge the viewer's perceptions of modern art.

Do not miss the panoramic **views★★★** *(from the top floor)* of the Thames and the city with St Paul's Cathedral as a counterpoint on the north bank which is linked to the museum by the striking **Millennium Bridge.** ■

Philippe GUERSAN/© ACSI

GREENWICH ★★★

■ Maritime Centre

Greenwich has been in the royal domain since King Alfred's time. Henry V's brother, Humphrey, Duke of Gloucester, first enclosed the park and transformed the manor into a castle which he named Bella Court. The Tudors preferred Greenwich to their other residences and Henry VIII, who was born there, extended the castle into a vast palace with a royal armoury; he also founded naval dockyards upstream at Deptford and downstream at Woolwich. During the Commonwealth the palace became derelict. The only building to survive was the Queen's House (*see below*).

After the Restoration, Charles II commissioned John Webb, a student of Inigo Jones, to build a King's House. William and Mary, who preferred Hampton Court, granted a charter for the foundation of a Royal Hospital for Seamen at Greenwich, with **Wren** as surveyor. In 1873 the Webb and Wren buildings were transformed into the Royal Naval College, while the Queen's House, extended by two wings in 1807, became the National Maritime Museum in 1937.

■ Queen's House ★★

This elegant white Palladian villa, which is part of the **National Maritime Museum ★★**, was commissioned by James I for his queen, Anne of Denmark, from Inigo Jones, who designed (1615) the first Classical mansion in England. Although work ceased on Anne's death it was resumed when Charles I gave the house to his Queen, Henrietta Maria, whose name appears on the north front along with the date 1635. Distinctive features include its colour, the beautiful horse-shoe

Dolphin Lamppost

© MICHELIN

shaped staircase descending from the terrace on the north front and the loggia on the south front facing the park.

■ Greenwich Park and Old Royal Observatory★

The Park, the oldest enclosed royal domain, extends for 180 acres/ 72ha, rising to a point 155ft/47m above the river, crowned by the Old Royal Observatory and the **General Wolfe** Monument. In 1675 Charles II directed Wren to "build a small observatory within our park at Greenwich, upon the highest ground at or near the place where the castle stood" for the "finding out of the longitude of places for perfect navigation and astronomy".

Inside Wren's brick **Flamsteed House** is the lofty Octagon Room, beautifully proportioned, equipped with what John Evelyn called "the choicest instrument". The **Meridian Building** was added in the mid-18C to house the growing **collection★★** of telescopes. Note Airey's Transit Circle, through which the meridian passes and outside, the brass meridian of O°, the clocks showing world times and the 24hr clock.

■ Old Royal Naval College★★

University of Greenwich campus. After demolishing the Tudor Palace, Wren retained the King Charles Block to which he added three symmetrical blocks named after King William, Queen Mary and Queen Anne. For the Queen's House he provided a river vista (150ft/46m) flanked by twin cupolas over the Chapel and the Painted Hall down to a new river embankment.

Millennium Dome

Riverside walks, parkland and lakes to attract wildlife have transformed the Greenwich peninsula where the site of a former gas works has been extensively redeveloped to include roads, housing, stores and other amenities for the local population. However, the focal point of the regenerated area is the Millennium Dome, a vast domed structure with a spectacular glass-fibre roof designed by Lord Richard Rogers, built to mark the third millennium. Owing to the lack of success of the Millennium Experience exhibition, the Dome has aroused much controversy and its future use is still uncertain.

The **Painted Hall*** in the domed refectory building is the work of **Sir James Thornhill**, exuberant Baroque representations of William and Mary, Anne, George I and his descendants, in an allegorical celebration of British maritime power, painted 1708-27. The **Chapel*** by Wren was redecorated after a fire in 1779 by "**Athenian**" **Stuart** and **William Newton** as a Rococo interior in Wedgwood pastels. In contrast to such deli-

cate patterns, at the apse is *St Paul after the Shipwreck at Malta* by **Benjamin West**, who designed the stone medallions for the pulpit which is made from the top of a three-decker pulpit.

■ **Cutty Sark****

Emphasising Greenwich's maritime importance, this splendid clipper, launched in 1869 for the

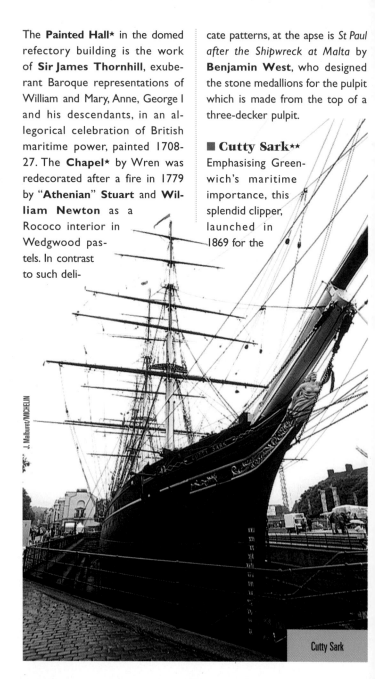

J. Malburet/MICHELIN

Cutty Sark

China tea trade, stands in a dry dock by the river. Famous in her heyday as the fastest clipper afloat, her best day's run, with all 32 000sq ft/ 3 000m² of canvas fully spread, was 363mi/584km. Beside her, the 53ft/ 16m **Gipsy Moth IV**, in which Sir Francis Chichester made his solo circumnavigation of the world in 1966-67, looks incredibly small.

There is a fine **view★★** of Greenwich Palace from Island Gardens on the north bank, which can be reached via the **foot tunnel** *(lift or 100 steps)*. ■

The gleaming cowls of the Thames Barrier

K. Brett/MICHELIN

Pagoda, Kew Gardens

Underground station:
Kew Gardens
Access to Kew to the south-west
of London is by A 4 or A 316 and
A 205 (South Circular)

KEW ★★★

■ **Kew Gardens**

The **Royal Botanic Gardens**, the finest in the land, were begun in 1756 by **Sir William Chambers** at the behest of Augusta, Princess of Wales. The same architect designed the **Orangery★**, the three small classical temples and in 1761 the ten-storey **Pagoda★** (163ft/50m high). As the gardens

Pioneering Work

Kew has practised biological control (Integrated Pest Management) throughout its premises tailored to 40 000 txa (specific species) of plant and 750 000 specimens of fungi since 1991. Efforts to save some of the world's rarest orchids have led scientists at Kew to evolve a way of germinating plants from seed without the symbiotic fungus required in more natural habitats. Some 5 000 species (about 20% of the total known number) are now propagated at Kew, having been accumulated over the last 200 years. The seed bank, founded to provide scientists and conservationists with the practical means of research, will expand at Wakehurst Place in West Sussex courtesy of the National Lottery.

grew, more buildings were added, notably Decimus Burton's **Palm House★★** in 1848. In 1899 Burton completed the **Temperate House★**, which contains camellias, rain forest and dragon trees. In 1987 Diana Princess of Wales opened the **Princess of Wales Conservatory**, a steel and glass diamond-shaped structure in which ten different tropical habitats ranging from mangrove

Palm House, Kew

swamp to sand desert are created and maintained by computer. A Japanese Minka House in the Bamboo Garden gives an insight into Japanese country life.

Close to the river stands **Kew Palace**** built for the London merchant Samuel Fortrey in 1631. The dark-red brick building with distinctive Dutch attic gables was leased by George II for Queen Caroline in about 1730 and purchased by George III in 1781. The interior is, therefore, that of a small country house of George III's time, with panelled rooms downstairs and intimate family portraits by Gainsborough, Zoffany and others upstairs.

Pleasant walks crisscross the grounds and the glories of Kew Gardens may be enjoyed in all seasons. ■

The Domesday Book

The famous register of lands of England, named after *Domus dei* – where the volumes were originally preserved in Winchester Cathedral, was commissioned by order of William the Conqueror so that he might ascertain the dues owed to him by his subjects, thereby setting the rules by which the monarch, later the government, might levy tax nationwide. As a result we have a comprehensive idea of how the kingdom was divided in 1085-86 both in terms of land holding and popular employment. Lords of the manor held the bulk of the land on a freehold basis, which they tenanted or leased to a complex hierarchy of dependents, villeins or freemen. Land was allocated to agricultural functions (meadow, pasture) in proportion to hunting (woodland) and fishing (ponds and rivers)...

The **Little Domesday** (384 pages) records estates throughout latter-day Essex, Norfolk and Suffolk, while the **Great Domesday** (450 pages) surveys the rest of the kingdom with the exception of Northumberland, Cumberland, Durham, parts of Lancashire and Westmorland which lay outside the king's jurisdiction. The City of London is also omitted as the conquering king could not have been certain of brokering his rights over the shrewd and powerful business community. A facsimile is displayed at the Public Record Office in Kew.

HAMPTON COURT★★★

This grand Tudor palace was begun (1514-29) by **Cardinal Wolsey**, son of an Ipswich butcher. He rose to high office but his failure to obtain papal approval for Henry VIII's divorce from Catherine of Aragon and the size and sumptuousness of his palace angered the King. He died in disgrace in 1530 a year after his fall from favour; Hampton Court was appropriated by the King.

Henry VIII then set about enlarging the palace; he built wings on the imposing west front, the splendid Great Hall with its hammerbeam roof and lavishly transformed the chapel. The remarkable Astronomical Clock in Clock Court, though

Overground train: Hampton Court from Waterloo
Hampton Court is to the south-west of London at the junction of A 308 and A 309

made for him in 1540, was brought here from St James's Palace in the 19C.

150 years after Henry's death, William and Mary had plans to rebuild the palace (which had survived Cromwell, having been reserved for him), but instead Wren began alterations in 1688. He rebuilt the east and south fronts, the **State Apartments** and the

Ph. Gajic/MICHELIN

smaller royal apartments. These rooms were decorated with carvings by **Grinling Gibbons** and painted ceilings by **Verrio**. The apartments and rooms contain a superb collection of **paintings** and **furniture**, while the **Kitchens** and the **King's Beer Cellars** and the **Wine Cellars** offer a glimpse of life in Tudor times.

The **Gardens***** as seen today are the results of various schemes. Charles II had the mile-long canal dug and William III created the Great Fountain Garden. The famous triangular **maze** north of the palace was planted in 1690. Further north, outside the palace walls, lies Bushy Park with its **Chestnut Avenue**, particularly colourful in May. In 1768 under George III, Capability Brown planted the **Great Vine***, now a plant of remarkable girth which produces an annual crop of 500-600 bunches of grapes *(on sale late Aug/early Sept)*. ■

Hampton Court

RICHMOND★★

Richmond, possessing what has been called the most beautiful urban green in England, grew to importance between the 12C and 17C as a royal seat and, after the Restoration, as the residential area of members of the court: Windsor, Hampton Court and Kew are easily accessible. In the courtiers' wake followed diplomats, politicians, professional men, dames and their schools, and with the coming of the railway in 1840, prosperous Victorian commuters.

🛈 *Old Town Hall, Whittaker Avenue, Richmond TW9 1TP. Open Mon-Sat, 10am-5pm; also May-Sep, Sun, 10.30am-1.30pm.* ☎ *020 8940 9125; Fax 020 8940 6899; information. services@richmond.gov.uk; www.richmond.gov.uk*

Richmond Palace: Royal Residence Through Six Reigns – The first residence, a manor house, erected in the 12C, was extended and embellished by **Edward III**, who died in it in 1377, was favoured by **Richard II**, his grandson while his queen, Anne of Bohemia, was alive but demolished at her death in 1394. A new palace, the second, was begun by **Henry V** but completed only 40 years after his death in the reign of **Edward IV** who gave it with the royal manor of Shene to his queen, Elizabeth Woodville, from whom it was confiscated by **Henry VII**; in 1499 it burned to the ground. Henry VII, parsimonious where his son was prodigal, nevertheless, "re-builded (the palace) again sumptuously and costly and changed the name of Shene and called it Richmond because his father and he were Earls of Rychmonde" (in Yorkshire). This palace, the third on the site, was to be the last.

The new Tudor palace conformed to standard design: service buildings of red brick, preserved today in the gateway, enclosed an outer or Base Court, now Old Palace Yard, from which a second gateway led to an inner or Middle Court, lined along one side by a Great Hall of stone with a lead roof.

The Privy Lodging, which included the state rooms, surrounded another court. Domed towers and turrets crowned the construction, which covered 10 acres/4ha and was by far the most splendid in the kingdom. **Henry VII** died in his palace; **Henry VIII** and Catherine of Aragon frequented it; **Queen Elizabeth** held court in it, particularly in springtime, and died there; Prince Henry, James I's son, resided there and added an art gallery to house the extensive collection of royal paintings, increased after the prince's death (in the palace) by the future **Charles I** who also re-sided there, notably during the plague of 1625. At the king's execution the palace was stripped and the contents, including the pictures, were sold. By the 18C little remained and private houses – the Old Palace, Gatehouse, Wardrobe, Trumpeters – were constructed out of the ruins on the site.

Richmond Theatre

Ph. Gajic/MICHELIN

■ Town Centre

On the east side of the main road are reminders of the growing village in the parish **Church of St Mary Magdalene** with its 16C square flint and stone tower, early brasses and monuments (actor Edmund Kean), 18C houses (Ormond and Halford Roads), 19C cottages (Waterloo Place), the Vineyard dating back in name to the 16C-17C when local vines were famous, and the rebuilt almshouses of 17C foundation – Queen **Elizabeth's**, **Bishop Duppa's** and **Michel's**. In Paradise Road stands Hogarth House built in 1748, where Leonard and **Virginia Woolf**, who lived there from 1915 to 1924, founded the **Hogarth Press**.

Cross the High St and pass through charming alleyways to Richmond Green.

■ Richmond Green

The Green, once the scene of Tudor jousting, has been a cricket pitch since the middle of the 17C.

Richmond Theatre, which overlooks the Little Green, was designed by Frank Matcham in 1889 and refurbished in 1991 more or less in accordance with its original appearance.

Along the east side of the Green are 17C and 18C houses and two narrow lanes opening into George Street. In the south corner in Paved Court are two pubs, the **Cricketers** and the **Prince's Head** *(see Directory)*; behind are narrow lanes with small shops.

Along the west side is **Old Palace Terrace** (1692-1700), six two-storey brick houses with straight hooded doorways, built by John Powell (who lived in n° 32 which he also built).

Oak House and **Old Palace Place** date back to 1700. **Old Friars** (1687 date on a rainwater head) is so named as it stands on part of the site of a monastery founded by Henry VII in 1500; the house was extended in the 18C to include a

concert room for the holding of "music mornings and evenings."

Maids of Honour Row*** – The famous row dates from 1724 when the future George II gave directions for "erecting a new building near his seat at Richmond to serve as lodgings for the Maids of Honour attending the Princess of Wales." There are four houses in all, each three storeys high with five bays apiece, pilastered, with friezed doorcases, and small gardens behind 18C wrought-iron gates and railings. The brick is mellow, the proportions perfect.

The Old Palace and the Gatehouse – On the south side are two houses: the first – castellated, bay-windowed and with a central doorway incorporating Tudor materials, notably brickwork, from Henry VII's palace; the second is the original outer gateway of the palace (note the restored arms of Henry VII over the arch).

The Wardrobe – *Old Palace Yard*. Note the blue diapered Tudor walls incorporated in the early 18C building, and the fine 18C ironwork.

Trumpeters' House* – *Old Palace Yard*. The main front of this house converted c 1701 from the Middle Gate of Richmond Palace, overlooks the garden and can be seen through the trees from the riverside path. The giant pedimented portico of paired columns was formerly guarded by stone statues after which the house is still named. For a brief period in 1848-49 it was occupied by Metternich.
Walk down Old Palace Lane.

■ Richmond Riverside

Old Palace Lane, lined by modest, wistaria-covered 19C houses and cottages, leads from the south-west corner of Richmond Green to the river.

Richmond Bridge★★ – The bridge, a classical, stone structure of five arches and parapet designed by James Paine, was built in 1774 to replace the horse ferry and widened in 1937; tolls were levied until the 19C. There is a milestone-obelisk at the north end.

The towpath continues beyond the bridge as a riverside promenade below Terrace Gardens (between Petersham Road and Richmond Hill).

From Richmond Bridge walk up Richmond Hill.

■ Richmond Hill

The **view★★** gets ever better as one climbs the steep road lined by balconied terraces, immortalised through the ages by many artists including Turner and Reynolds.

At the top, overlooking the park stands **Ancaster House**, a brick mansion with big bow windows, built in 1722 principally to designs

© Visit London

by **Robert Adam**. The house is now attached to the **Star and Garter Home** for disabled sailors, soldiers and airmen opposite, which stands on the site of an inn famous in the 18C and 19C and was opened in 1924. (The British Legion poppy factory is at the Richmond end of Petersham Road.)

The park gates which mark the hilltop are dated 1700 and are attributed to **"Capability" Brown**.

■ Richmond Park**

The countryside had been a royal chase for centuries when **Charles I** enclosed 2 470 acres/494ha as a park in 1637. It is the largest of the royal parks, and is famous for its varied **wildlife** – most notably its herds of almost tame red and fallow deer, its majestic **oak trees** and the **spring flowers** (rhododendrons) of the Isabella Plantation.

Among the houses in the park are **Pembroke Lodge** *(cafeteria)*, a rambling late-17C-18C house at the centre of colourful walled and woodland gardens adapted by **John Soane** from a molecatcher's cottage and later used by Lord John Russell (Prime Minister 1846-51 and 1865-66) and his grandson, the philosopher **Bertrand Russell**; Thatched House Lodge, the home of Princess Alexandra; and **White Lodge**, built by George II in 1727 as a hunting lodge and since 1955 the junior section of the **Royal Ballet School**. ■

ADDITIONAL SIGHTS

■ London Zoo★★

Regent's Park – ⊖ Camden Town.
The London Zoological Society opened on a 5 acre/2ha site in Regent's Park in 1828, at the instigation of Sir Stamford Raffles. Today the Zoo has spread to cover 36 acres/14ha and has a staff of more than 100 caring for approximately 8 000 animals of 900 species.

Many new and innovative buildings have been constructed to house the animals, and the emphasis is now placed on breeding endangered animals and on foreign conservation projects.

■ Kenwood House★★ (The Iveagh Bequest)

Hampstead Lane – Access by bus 210 from Golders Green or Archway.
William Murray, younger son of a

Scottish peer, acquired Kenwood, a 50-year-old brick house on the north side of Hampstead Heath, in 1754, two years before becoming Lord Chief Justice and Earl of Mansfield.

In 1764 he invited fellow Scot **Robert Adam** to enlarge and embellish the house. Adam transformed it, outside and in, leaving a strong imprint of his style. Particularly notable are the **Library★★** and the very fine collection of paintings. A sensitive redecoration scheme has enhanced the refined atmosphere of this elegant house.

■ Osterley Park★★

⊖ *Osterley Park.* Osterley is the place to see **Robert Adam** interior decoration at its most complete – room after room just as he designed them, in every detail from ceilings and walls to the furniture. What had started life as a

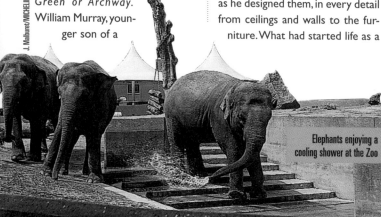

Elephants enjoying a
cooling shower at the Zoo

J. Malburet/MICHELIN

late-15C Tudor brick manor house was transformed into a mansion by Sir Thomas Gresham, founder of the Royal Exchange, in 1562.

In 1711 the mansion was purchased by Francis Child, a clothier's son from Wiltshire who had made his fortune as a City banker. He was 69 when he bought Osterley and never lived there. It was his grandson, Francis, who commissioned Adam to transform the mansion, achieving between 1761 and 1780 the rich interior we admire today.

■ Syon Park★★

Overground train to Syon Park station from Waterloo. The colonnaded east front is visible across the river from Kew Gardens. The Lord Protector, Duke of Somerset, built a Tudor mansion on the site of a former monastery, given to him by his nephew Edward VI in 1547; five years later he was charged with treason and executed. During the next hundred years many owners of the house were beheaded and when, in less troubled times, the house passed to Hugh Percy, 1st Earl of

Northumberland, in 1762, he felt it needed remodelling. **Robert Adam** richly ornamented and furnished the house, while **Capability Brown** redesigned the gardens and extended them to the river. A number of notable Stuart portraits by Van Dyck, Lely and others further embellish the interior.

■ Ham House★★

Overground train to Twickenham from Waterloo. This is an exquisite three-storey brick house dating from 1610 which was enlarged in the 1670s by Elizabeth Dysart and her second husband, the Duke of Lauderdale. Much of their original furnishing has survived, lavish even by the standards of the age. The house is rich in ornate plasterwork on the ceilings and splendid carved wood panelling on the walls. The **Great Staircase** of 1637, built of oak around a square well and gilded, has a beautiful balustrade of boldly carved trophies of arms. Notable among the many fine Dutch, English and Italian paintings are portraits by Lely, Kneller and Reynolds, including ladies at Charles II's Court – young, fair, delicately complexioned and far from innocent.

■ Chiswick House★

Burlington Lane, Chiswick – ⊖ *Turnham Green and Bus 190.* A Jacobean mansion was purchased by the 1st Earl of Burlington in 1682. On his return from his second Grand Tour (1714-19) the 3rd Earl, Richard Boyle (1695-1753) designed a Palladian villa (1727-29) to display his works of art and to entertain his friends. **William Kent** (1686-1748), a follower of Inigo Jones, was responsible for much of the interior decoration and the gardens.

The lower floor – octagon hall, lobbies and library – now displays engravings, sculptures and other material about the creation and restoration of the house and garden. On the principal floor the **Dome Saloon**, its eight walls punctuated by gold-highlighted doors and Classical busts, rises by way of an ochre entablature to a windowed drum and diamond-patterned dome.

■ Madame Tussaud's★

Marylebone – ⊖ *Baker Street.* The famous waxworks include the French royal family, made by Madame Tussaud herself, statesmen of several ages and countries, modern celebrities in the worlds of sport and entertainment, criminals and murderers at the scene of their crimes as well as a brief

Great Conservatory, Syon Park

K. Brett/MICHELIN

dark ride through the history of London.

■ Docklands*

London's docks were built in the early 19C to serve the massive trade passing through the world's largest port. Cargo ships brought in tobacco, spices, rice, wine, spirits, timber – and later, in the new refrigerated vessels, fruit, meat and grain before setting sail again with the products of Britain's booming manufacturing industries. The scene was set for 150 years of activity.

The 1960s and 1970s brought a sharp decline, and one by one the docks closed as new berths, equipped for modern container vessels, were built downriver. In 1960, there were jobs for 50 000 dockers. By 1985, only 3 000 remained, and 200 000 more jobs in dock-dependent businesses had vanished.

From the mid-1980s onwards a massive redevelopment programme totally transformed Docklands. Aided by relaxed planning laws and substantial financial inducements, property developers found rich pickings in creating a new city to the east.

The largest projects were created on the Isle of Dogs, on the Thames' north bank, so named because hunting dogs were kept there. Development in Surrey Docks, on the south side, was on a more human scale, with more housing, especially for local residents. As well as over one million square metres of office space, almost 20 000 homes have been built and extensive leisure facilities, mostly water-based, created. The result is an exciting, modernistic but at times, alienating business environment, built in a variety of architectural styles.

The Island Gardens branch of the Docklands Light Railway (DLR) provides dramatic views as it swoops through the Isle of Dogs, often on stilts and crossing the three West India Docks on slender bridges. The first view of the water comes after Limehouse station; there is a marina in Limehouse Basin, and along the river are some 18C merchants' houses. Near Westferry station, the handsome Dockmaster's House has been converted into a restaurant.

Ahead is the huge **Canary Wharf Complex★★**, the centrepiece of Docklands – if only by virtue of its size. Even the station, set under a vast canopy (most of the other DLR stations are bare platforms), seems cathedral-like. The office buildings are grouped around Cabot Square, where the computer-controlled fountain can perform 42 different water 'dances'.

There are shops and restaurants at ground-floor and basement levels. Canary Wharf Tower – officially N° 1 Canada Square – is visible from well outside London. At 272m/824ft, it is the tallest building in Britain and the second tallest in Europe. There are 50 storeys, 1.3 million square feet of office space, and 32 passenger lifts.

Crossharbour is the station for the London Arena, used for concerts and sports events, and for Millwall Dock, where great cranes stand along the water's edge, silent witnesses to history. Glengall Bridge is a swing bridge which admits craft to the dock near the entrance to the Thames; here, housing and small-scale offices are intermixed pleasingly.

Island Gardens station is close to the Thames. There are majestic views of Greenwich, which is reached by a foot tunnel. ■

Canary Wharf

© LDDC

PRACTICAL
INFORMATION

■ Planning a trip ■

Take a look at www.visit.london.com when planning your trip to London.

Tourist Information Centre – London Tourist Board Information Centres at Heathrow, Terminals 1, 2, 3 and Underground Station Concourse and at main railway stations (Liverpool Street, Victoria and Waterloo International).

The Britain Visitor Centre, 1 Lower Regent Street, SW1Y 4NS (personal callers only), ☎ 020 8846 9000; BVCCustomerServices@bta.org.uk

City of London Information Centre, St Paul's Churchyard, EC4. ☎ 020 7332 1456; Fax 020 7332 1457

Pepys House, 2 Cutty Sark Gardens, Greenwich SE10 9LW ☎ 0870 608 2000; Fax 020 8853 4607; tic@greenwich.gov.uk

Old Town Hall, Whittaker Avenue, Richmond, Surrey TW9 1TP ☎ 020 8940 9125; Fax 020 8332 0802; information.services@richmond.gov.uk

■ Getting around ■

London Pass – This pass, which is valid for public transport, over 50 attractions and other facilities, is available from the TIC and can also be purchased abroad. ☎ 0870 242 9988; www.londonpass.com

Public Transport – Zoned tube and bus tickets are sold singly on buses or at underground stations. There are various options: Carnets of 10 tickets for travel by underground within Zone 1, Travelcards valid for 1 day, Weekend passes, 7-day Weekly, Family Travelcards. Transport for London Enquiries, 55 Broadway, SW1H 0DB. ☎ 020 7222 1234.

Congestion Charging – A £5 charge per day is levied on all vehicles (except motor cycles and exempt vehicles) entering the central zone between 7am and 6.30pm – Mon-Fri except Bank Hols. Payment can be made in advance, or on the day, by post, on the Internet, by telephone or at retail outlets. A charge of up to £80 will be made for non-payment. Further information is available on the Transport for London website – www.tfl.gov.uk

■ Sightseeing ■

Tours on open-topped buses start from Victoria, Green Park, Piccadilly, Coventry Street, Trafalgar Square, Haymarket, Lower Regent Street, Marble Arch, Baker Street, Tower Hill. Some tours are non-stop; some allow passengers to hop on or off and continue on a later bus. Ticket prices vary.

For guided walking tours consult the London Tourist Board or press listings (*Time Out*).

Thames cruises start from Westminster Pier, Charing Cross Pier, Tower Pier, Greenwich Pier. 24hr recorded message for the London Tourist Board Riverboat Information Service: ☎ 09064 123 432 or contact service points direct. Evening cruises with music and/or a meal are also available (details in *Time Out*).

The **London Waterbus Company** runs a regular service along the Regent's Canal; www.londonwaterbus.co.uk; ☎ 020 7482 2660 (information), 020 7482 2550 (bookings). Also Jason's Trip ☎ 0020 7286 3428; Fax 020 7266 2656; enquiries@jasons.co.uk; www.jasons.co.uk; and Jenny Wren ☎ 020 7485 4433; Fax 020 7485 9098; www.walkersquay.com

Frog Tours operates an unusual tour (60-70min, Jun-Oct) by road and river on board an amphibious vehicle with live commentary, starting from County Hall (near Westminster Bridge). ☎ 020 7928 3132; Fax 0207 928 2050; enquiries@frogtours.com; www.frogtours.com

British Airways London Eye offers panoramic views of London. ☎ 0870 5000 600; customer.services@ba-londoneye.com; www.ba-londoneye.com

The London Tourist Board provides maps (charge) of the **Silver Jubilee Walkway** (10mi/16km) with eight viewpoints with indicators identifying neighbouring buildings.

■ Shopping ■

Visit Knightsbridge (Harrods, Harvey Nichols), Bond Street (fashion, antiques), Oxford and Regent Streets (department stores), King's Road (boutiques, antiques), Kensington High Street (large stores and boutiques), Covent Garden (boutiques and crafts), Piccadilly (gentlemen's outfitters, sportswear)

■ Entertainment ■

Theatres, cinemas, nightclubs and music venues are to be found in the area around Leicester Square, Piccadilly and Covent Garden. Consult the daily press *(Evening Standard)* or *Time Out* (published Wednesdays) for listings. Theatre Tokens accepted at over 160 theatres nationwide including all London West End theatres can be purchased from WH Smith, Hammicks Bookshops, Books etc and all participating theatres or from Ticketmaster ☎ 020 7344 4444 or TOKENLINE ☎ 020 7240 8800.

tkts, Leicester Square, the only official Half-Price and Discount theatre booth in London, offers a limited number of half-price tickets to most West End shows on the day of performance. They are available on a first-come-first-served basis, cash/credit card payment only accepted plus service charge, no returns, maximum four tickets per application. Open Mon-Sat, 10am-7pm; Sun for matinées only noon-3.30pm. ☎ 020 7557 6700; Fax 020 7557 6799; enquiries@solttma.co.uk; www.officiallondontheatre.co.uk

■ Where to Stay and Where to Eat ■

HOTELS

Compared with other European cities, London is an expensive place to stay. Finding a suitable room in a metropolis with over 13 million visitors annually and an average hotel occupancy rate of 80%, often requires patience. Fortunately, the choice of accommodation is astounding – nearly 130 000 beds in London alone – and with proper preparation prior to your trip, you will undoubtedly find pleasant accommodation in your price range and in your favourite area. Bear in mind that advance reservation is a must in any season, especially during the school holidays (Christmas, Easter and June to September).

The two rates quoted for each establishment refer to the nightly rate of a single or double room. Breakfast may not always be included in the price.

Bromley

Melrose House – 89 Lennard Rd, Penge, SE20 7LY – ☎ (020) 8776 8884 – melrose.hotel@virgin.net – £40-£85. An imposing Victorian house with a conservatory sitting room. Breakfast is taken "en famille" and the older bedrooms still have their original fireplaces.

Camden

London Euston Travel Inn Capital – 141 Euston Rd, Euston, WC1H 9PJ – ☎ (0870) 2383301 – £79.95. Budget accommodation with clean and spacious bedrooms, all with a large workspace. Double glazed but still ask for a quieter room at the back.

Langorf – 20 Frognal, Hampstead, NW3 6AG – ☎ (020) 7794 4483 – info@langorfhotel.com – £82-£110. Converted Edwardian house in a quiet residential area. Bright breakfast room overlooks secluded walled garden. Fresh bedrooms, many of which have high ceilings.

Swiss Cottage – 4 Adamson Rd, Swiss Cottage, NW3 3HP – ☎ (020) 7722 2281 – reservations@swisscottagehotel.co.uk – £66-£120. Made up of four Victorian houses in a residential conservation area. Bedrooms vary in size and shape, reflecting the age of the house. Basement breakfast room.

Enfield

Oak Lodge – 80 Village Rd, Bush Hill Park, Enfield, EN1 2EU – ☎ (020) 8360 7082 – oaklodge@fsmail.net – £69.50-£89.50. An Edwardian house personally run by the hospitable owner and located in a residential area. Individually decorated bedrooms are compact but well-equipped. Cosy dining room overlooks secluded rear garden.

Haringey

Mountview – 31 Mount View Rd, Crouch End, N4 4SS – ☎ (020) 8340 9222 – mountviewbb@aol.com – £40-£70. Redbrick Victorian house with a warm and stylish ambience engendered by the homely décor. One bedroom features an original fireplace and two overlook the quiet rear garden.

Hillingdon

Travel Inn Heathrow Capital – 15 Bath Rd, Heathrow Airport, TW6 2AB – ☎ (0870) 6075075 – £69.95. Well-priced Travel Inn with modern, wood-panelled exterior and huge atrium. Well-equipped meeting rooms. Bedrooms are of good quality with triple glazing. Bright, airy, informal grill restaurant.

Islington

The Rookery – 12 Peters Lane, Cowcross St, Clerkenwell, EC1M 6DS – ☎ (020) 7336 0931 – reservations@rookery.co.uk – £252.60-£323.10. A row of charmingly restored 18C houses. Wood panelling, stone-flagged flooring, open fires and antique furniture. Highly individual bedrooms, with Victorian bathrooms.

Kensington and Chelsea

L'Hotel – 28 Basil St, Chelsea, SW3 1AS – ☎ (020) 7589 6286 – reservations@lhotel.co.uk – £116.30-£188. Discreet town house a short walk from Harrods. Wooden shutters, pine furniture and stencilled walls provide a subtle rural theme. Well-appointed, comfy and informally run. Basement café dining.

Twenty Nevern Square – Nevern Sq, Earl's Court, SW5 9PD – ☎ (020) 7565 9555 – hotel@twentynevernsquare.co.uk – £110-£140. In an attractive Victorian garden square, an individually designed, privately owned town house. Original pieces of furniture and some rooms with their own terrace.

Mayflower – 26-28 Trebovir Rd, Earl's Court, SW5 9NJ – ☎ (020) 7370 0991 – mayflowerhotel@mayflower-group.co.uk – £69-£99. Two white houses combined into a stylish establishment with secluded rear garden, juice bar and breakfast room. Highly individual bedrooms with Indian and Asian décor.

Henley House – 30 Barkston Gdns, Earl's Court, SW5 0EN – ☎ (020) 7370 4111 – reservations@henleyhousehotel.com – £74-£89. Located in a pleasant redbricked square, just yards from the high street. Bedrooms all styled similarly, with floral designs and good extras. Conservatory breakfast room.

Amsterdam – 7 and 9 Trebovir Rd, Earl's Court, SW5 9LS – ☏ (020) 7370 2814 – reservations@amsterdam-hotel.com – £72-£86. Basement breakfast room and a small secluded garden. The boldly decorated bedrooms dazzle with vivid colour schemes; some boast their own balcony.

Rushmore – 11 Trebovir Rd, Earl's Court, SW5 9LS – ☏ (020) 7370 3839 – rushmore-reservations@london.com – £59-£79. Behind its Victorian façade lies an hotel popular with tourists. Individually decorated bedrooms in a variety of shapes and sizes. Piazza-styled conservatory breakfast room.

Holland Court – 31-33 Holland Rd, Kensington, W14 8HJ – ☏ (020) 7371 1133 – reservations@hollandcourt.com – £95-£125. Privately owned and run terraced house. Pretty little garden next to the conservatory extension of the breakfast room. Well-kept bedrooms benefit from the large windows.

Portobello – 22 Stanley Gdns, North Kensington, W11 2NG – ☏ (020) 7727 2777 – info@portobello-hotel.co.uk – £120-£275. An attractive Victorian town house in an elegant terrace. Original and theatrical décor. Circular beds, half-testers, Victorian baths: no two bedrooms are the same.

Five Sumner Place – 5 Sumner Pl, South Kensington, SW7 3EE – ☏ (020) 7584 7586 – reservations@sumnerplace.com – £100-£152. Part of a striking white terrace built in 1848 in this fashionable part of town. Breakfast served in bright conservatory. Good sized bedrooms.

Aster House – 3 Sumner Pl, South Kensington, SW7 3EE – ☏ (020) 7581 5888 – asterhouse@btinternet.com – £100-£190. End of terrace Victorian house with a pretty little rear garden and first floor conservatory. Ground floor rooms available. A wholly non-smoking establishment.

Lambeth

London County Hall Travel Inn Capital – Belvedere Rd, Waterloo, SE1 7PB – ☏ (0870) 2383300 – london.county.hall.mti@whitbread.com – £82.95. Adjacent to the London Eye and within the County Hall building. Budget accommodation in a central London location that is the envy of many, more expensive, hotels.

Richmond-upon-Thames

Chase Lodge – 10 Park Rd, Hampton Wick, KT1 4AS – ☏ (020) 8943 1862 – info@chaselodgehotel.com – £65-£105. Personally-run small hotel in mid-terrace Victorian property in an area of outstanding architectural and historical interest. Individually furnished, comfortable rooms. Bright, airy conservatory restaurant.

Doughty Cottage – 142A Richmond Hill, Richmond, TW10 6RN – ✆ (020) 8332 9434 – deniseoneill425@aol.co.uk – £75-£103. Positioned high above the river, this attractive 18C Regency house is discreetly set behind a picturesque walled garden. Thoughtfully equipped rooms, two with patio gardens.

Southwark

Southwark Rose – 43-47 Southwark Bridge Rd, Southwark, SE1 9HH – ✆ (020) 7015 1480 – info@southwarkrosehotel.co.uk – £105. Purpose built budget hotel south of the City, near the Globe Theatre. Top floor breakfast room with bar. Uniform style, reasonably spacious bedrooms with writing desks.

Sutton

Thatched House – 135-141 Cheam Rd, Sutton, SM1 2BN – ✆ (020) 8642 3131 – thatchedhouse@btconnect.com – £85-£100. Part thatched and gabled private hotel on busy main road just out of the town centre. Most comfortable and quietest rooms overlook the pretty gardens. Rustic-styled dining room.

Westminster (City of)

Delmere – 130 Sussex Gdns, Bayswater and Maida Vale, W2 1UB – ✆ (020) 7706 3344 – delmerehotel@compuserve.com – £86-£107. Attractive stucco fronted and porticoed Victorian property. Now a friendly private hotel. Compact bedrooms are both well-equipped and kept. Modest prices. Bright, relaxed restaurant and adjacent bar.

Miller's – 111A Westbourne Grove, Bayswater and Maida Vale, W2 4UW – ✆ (020) 7243 1024 – enquiries@millersuk.com – £188-£264. Victorian house brimming with antiques and knick-knacks. Charming sitting room provides the setting for a relaxed breakfast. Individual, theatrical rooms named after poets.

Byron – 36-38 Queensborough Terr, Bayswater and Maida Vale, W2 3SH – ✆ (020) 7243 0987 – byron@capricornhotels.co.uk – £75-£120. Centrally located and refurbished in the late 1990's-an ideal base for tourists. Bright and modern bedrooms are generally spacious and all have showers en suite.

Hart House – 51 Gloucester Pl, Regent's Park and Marylebone, W1U 8JF – ✆ (020) 7935 2288 – reservations@harthouse.co.uk – £70-£105. Once home to French nobility escaping the 1789 Revolution. Now an attractive Georgian, mid-terraced private hotel. Warm and welcoming service. Well kept bedrooms.

St George – 49 Gloucester Pl, Regent's Park and Marylebone, W1U 8JE – ✆ (020) 7486 8586 – reservations@stgeorge-hotel.net – £95-£135. Terraced house on a busy street, usefully located within walking distance of many attractions. Offers a warm welcome and comfortable bedrooms which are spotlessly maintained.

Hazlitt's – 6 Frith St, Soho, W1D 3JA – ☎ (020) 7434 1771 – reservations@hazlitts.co.uk – £205.60-£240.80. A row of three adjoining early 18c town houses and former home of the eponymous essayist. Individual and charming bedrooms, many with antique furniture and Victorian baths.

Tophams Belgravia – 28 Ebury St, Victoria, SW1W 0LU – ☎ (020) 7730 8147 – tophams_belgravia@compuserve.com – £115-£170. Family owned and run since 1937, this hotel has a certain traditional charm. Cosy lounges, roaring fires and antique furniture aplenty. Individually decorated bedrooms. Homely basement dining room.

Winchester – 17 Belgrave Rd, Victoria, SW1V 1RB – ☎ (020) 7828 2972 – winchesterhotel17@hotmail.com – £85-£100. Behind the portico entrance one finds a friendly, well-kept private hotel. The generally spacious rooms are pleasantly appointed. Comprehensive English breakfast offered.

RESTAURANTS

London has become a gourmet's paradise, and the capital now occupies a prominent role on the international culinary scene. The number and variety of eating places reflect the multitude of current cooking styles ranging from traditional British (including fish and chips), to classic French, to the now-popular Mediterranean-style and world cuisine from far-flung places around the globe. Indeed, a tasty legacy of the British Empire's former worldwide ties is the abundance of dishes hailing from South Asia, Africa, the Caribbean and the Near and Far East.

Like the hotel listings, the restaurants recommended in this guide have been carefully selected for quality, atmosphere, location and value for money.

The two prices given for each establishment represent a minimum and maximum price for a full meal excluding beverages.

Barnet

Philpott's Mezzaluna – 424 Finchley Rd, Child's Hill, NW2 2HY – ☎ (020) 7794 0455 – £19-£23. Homely Italian restaurant, affably run by patrons. Huge lunar artefacts complement the plain walls. Weekly changing menus offer tasty, modern cuisine at moderate prices.

Brent

Sabras – 263 High Rd, Willesden Green, NW10 2RX – ☎ (020) 8459 0340 – £15.50-£22. Inexpensive Indian vegetarian food served in modest, but friendly, surroundings. Framed awards and write-ups garnered since opening in 1973 bear testament to its popularity.

Camden

Passione – 10 Charlotte St, Bloomsbury, W1T 2LT – ☎ (020) 7636 2833 – liz@passione.co.uk – £31-£42. Compact but light and airy. Modern Italian cooking served in informal surroundings, with friendly and affable service. Particularly busy at lunchtime.

The Wells – 30 Well Walk, Hampstead, NW3 1BX – ☎ (020) 7794 3785 – £23.75-£31. Attractive 18C inn with modern interior. Ground floor bar and a few tables next to open-plan kitchen; upstairs more formal dining rooms. Classically-based French cooking.

The Magdala – 2A South Hill Park, Hampstead, NW3 2SB – ☎ (020) 7435 2503 – £15.70-£24.25. Located on the edge of the Heath. Two bars popular with locals, one with open-plan kitchen. Upstairs dining room, open at weekends, offers robust cooking. Simpler lunch menu.

The Queens – 49 Regent's Park Rd, Primrose Hill, NW1 8XD – ☎ (020) 7586 0408 – £16.90-£21.90. One of the original "gastropubs". Very popular balcony overlooking Primrose Hill and the high street. Robust and traditional cooking from the blackboard menu.

The Engineer – 65 Gloucester Ave, Primrose Hill, NW1 8JH – ☎ (020) 7722 0950 – info@the-eng.com – £25.25-£29.25. Busy pub that boasts a warm, neighbourhood feel. Dining room, decorated with modern pictures, has modish appeal. Informal, chatty service. Modern cuisine.

Junction Tavern – 101 Fortess Rd, Tufnell Park, NW5 1AG – ☎ (020) 7485 9400 – £16.50-£25. Typical Victorian pub with wood panelling. Eat in the bar or in view of the open plan kitchen. Robust cooking using good fresh ingredients, served in generous portions.

Ealing

Ealing Park Tavern – 222 South Ealing Rd, South Ealing, W5 4RL – ☎ (020) 8758 1879 – £18.50-£22. Victorian building with an atmospheric, cavernous interior. Characterful beamed dining room and an open-plan kitchen serving modern dishes from a daily changing menu.

Enfield

The Kings Head – 1 The Green, Winchmore Hill, N21 1BB – ☎ (020) 8886 1988 – £16.90-£23.90. Large scrubbed pine tables, leather sofas and wall tapestries decorate this contemporary inn. Modern, eclectic cooking with supplementary blackboard specials.

Hackney

Rasa – 55 Stoke Newington Church St, Stoke Newington, N16 0AR – ☎ (020) 7249 0344 – £10.25-£13.75. Busy Indian restaurant, an unpretentious environment in which to sample authentic, sometimes unusual, dishes. The "Feast" offers a taste of the range of foods on offer.

Hammersmith and Fulham

Zinc – Fulham Island, 1 Farm Lane, Fulham, SW6 1BE – ☎ (020) 7386 2250 – £15-£30.50. Bright modern bar; informal chic restaurant. Grills, seafood and modern international fare. No bookings accepted for the heated terrace so arrive early for a table.

The Salisbury Tavern – 21 Sherbrooke Rd, Fulham, SW6 7HX – ☎ (020) 7381 4005 – thesalisburytavern@longshotplc.com – £17.50-£26.70. Its residential location attracts a local crowd to the stylish bar. Separate, and equally à la mode, dining room with pleasant young staff. Wide ranging traditional menu.

Anglesea Arms – 35 Wingate Rd, Hammersmith, W6 0UR – ☎ (020) 8749 1291 – £12.95-£21.95. The laid-back atmosphere and local feel make this pub a popular venue. Worth arriving early as bookings are not taken. Modern cooking from blackboard menu.

Havelock Tavern – 57 Masbro Rd, Shepherd's Bush, W14 0LS – ☎ (020) 7603 5374 – £19.50-£23.50. Typical new wave London pub where the kitchen produces generously portioned modern food. Pine tables and chairs, and a large central bar. Privately owned.

Hounslow

The Bollo – 13-15 Bollo Lane, Chiswick, W4 5LS – ☎ (020) 8994 6037 – £14.50-£28.50. Attractive period brick pub with dining area under a domed glass rotunda. Daily changing menu-mixture of traditional and eclectic dishes-served throughout the pub.

Islington

The Parsee – 34 Highgate Hill, Archway, N19 5NL – ☎ (020) 7272 9091 – dining@theparsee.co.uk – £19.40-£22.70. Two brightly painted rooms, one non smoking and featuring a painting of a Parsee Angel. Good value, interesting, carefully spiced cuisine, Persian and Indian in inspiration.

St John's – 91 Junction Rd, Archway, N19 5QU – ☎ (020) 7272 1587 – stjohnsarchway@virgin.net – £15.50-£25. Busy front bar enjoys a lively atmosphere; dining room in a large rear room. Log fire at one end, open hatch into kitchen the other. Blackboard menu; rustic cooking.

Centuria – 100 St Paul's Rd, Canonbury, N1 2QP – ☎ (020) 7704 2345 – £20.25-£23.50. Large pub in a residential area, with the dining room separate from the busy bar. Open-plan kitchen produces a modern menu, with influences ranging from Italy to Morocco.

Quality Chop House – 94 Farringdon Rd, Finsbury, EC1R 3EA – ☎ (020) 7837 5093 – qualitychophouse@clara.co.uk – £17.75-£28. On the window is etched "Progressive working class caterers". This is borne out with the individual café-style booths and a menu ranging from jellied eels to caviar.

The Peasant – 240 St John St, Finsbury, EC1V 4PH – ☎ (020) 7336 7726 – eat@thepeasant.co.uk – £21-£27. Large, busy pub with half of the ground floor given over as a bar. Dining continues in the high-ceilinged room upstairs. Robust and rustic cooking with generous portions.

Drapers Arms – 44 Barnsbury St, Islington, N1 1ER – ☎ (020) 7619 0348 – £18.50-£29. Real presence to the the façade of this Georgian pub tucked away in a quiet residential area. Spacious modern interior where competent, contemporary dishes are served.

The Northgate – 113 Southgate Rd, Islington, N1 3JS – ☎ (020) 7359 7392 – £20-£25. Corner pub with wood flooring and modern art on display. Rear dining area with a large blackboard menu offering a cross section of internationally influenced modern dishes.

The Social – 33 Linton St, Islington, N1 7DU – ☎ (020) 7354 5809 – £15.50-£25. The former Hanbury Arms has a youthful clientele attracted by the DJ and music in the bar. The open plan kitchen and restaurant serve from a modern, sensibly priced menu.

The Barnsbury – 209-211 Liverpool Rd, Islington, N1 1LX – ☎ (020) 7607 5519 – info@thebarnsbury.co.uk – £17.50-£26.45. Former public house with pine tables and chairs arranged round central counter bar; art work for sale on the walls. Robust and hearty food in generous portions.

Kensington and Chelsea

Bibendum Oyster Bar – Michelin House, 81 Fulham Rd, Chelsea, SW3 6RD – ☎ (020) 7589 1480 – manager@bibendum.co.uk – £19-£29. Dine in either the busy bar, or in the light and relaxed foyer of this striking landmark. Concise menu of mainly cold dishes focusing on fresh seafood and shellfish.

itsu – 118 Draycott Ave, Chelsea, SW3 3AE – ☎ (020) 7590 2400 – cebsonetcomuk@co.uk – £15-£20. Sit at the conveyor belt and select your dishes from it. Cosmopolitan 'euro sushi' selection with Asian specialities. Fashionable and willing staff. Busy bar upstairs.

Admiral Codrington – 17 Mossop St, Chelsea, SW3 2LY – ☎ (020) 7581 0005 – theadmiralcodrington@longshotplc.com – £19.85-£27.95. Aproned staff offer attentive, relaxed service in this busy gastropub. A retractable roof provides alfresco dining in the modern back room. Cosmopolitan menu of modern dishes.

Chelsea Ram – 32 Burnaby St, Chelsea, SW10 0PL – ☎ (020) 7351 4008 – pint@chelsearam.com – £17-£24. Wooden floors, modern artwork and books galore feature in this forever popular pub. Concise menu of modern British cooking with daily changing specials. Friendly atmosphere.

Swag and Tails – 10-11 Fairholt St, Chelsea, SW7 1EG – ☎ (020) 7584 6926 – swagandtails@mway.com – £17.90-£28. Attractive Victorian pub close to Harrods and the fashionable Knightsbridge shops. Polite and approachable service of a blackboard menu of light snacks and seasonal dishes.

Builders Arms – 13 Britten St, Chelsea, SW3 3TY – ☎ (020) 7349 9040 – £18.40-£25. Modern 'gastropub' favoured by the locals. Eclectic menu of contemporary dishes with blackboard specials. Polite service from a young and eager team.

Lots Road Pub & Dining Room – 114 Lots Rd, Chelsea, SW10 0RJ – ☎ (020) 7352 6645 – lotsroad@thespiritgroup.com – £16-£25. Traditional corner pub with an open-plan kitchen, flowers at each table and large modern pictures on the walls. Contemporary menus change daily.

Zaika – 1 Kensington High St, Kensington, W8 5NP – ☎ (020) 7795 6533 – info@zaika-restaurant.co.uk – £17.95-£46.25. A converted bank, sympathetically restored, with original features and Indian artefacts. Well organised service; careful and accomplished modern Indian cooking.

Malabar – 27 Uxbridge St, Kensington, W8 7TQ – ☎ (020) 7727 8800 – feedback@malabar-restaurant.co.uk – £14.75-£28.50. Indian restaurant in a residential street. Three rooms with individual personalities and informal service. Extensive range of good value dishes, particularly vegetarian.

Merton

The Fire Stables – 27-29 Church Rd, Wimbledon, SW19 5DQ – ☎ (020) 8946 3197 – thefirestables@thespiritgroup.com – £18.25-£29. Modern "gastropub" in village centre. Open-plan kitchen. Polished wood tables and banquettes. Varied modern British dishes. Expect fishcakes, duck confit salad or risotto.

Richmond-upon-Thames

Brula – 43 Crown Rd, St Margarets, Twickenham, TW1 3EJ – ☎ (020) 8892 0602 – £11-£25. Behind the stained glass windows and the rose arched entrance, you'll find an intimate and cosy bistro. Friendly and relaxed service of a weekly changing, rustic menu.

Ma Cuisine – 6 Whitton Rd, Twickenham, TW1 1BJ – ☎ (020) 8607 9849 – £9.50-£15. Small neighbourhood bistro style restaurant offering good value. Classic French country cooking with blackboard specials; concise wine list.

Southwark

Tate Cafe (7th Floor) – Tate Modern, Bankside, Southwark, SE1 9TE – ☎ (020) 7401 5020 – £19.75-£26.50. Modernity to match the museum, with vast murals and huge windows affording stunning views. Canteen-style menu at a sensible price with obliging service.

Westminster (City Of)

The Vale – 99 Chippenham Rd, Bayswater and Maida Vale, W9 2AB – ☎ (020) 7266 0990 – thevale@hotmail.com – £12-£25. Dine in either the light and spacious conservatory, or in the original bar of this converted pub. Modern British food with Mediterranean influences. Destination bar below.

L'Accento – 16 Garway Rd, Bayswater and Maida Vale, W2 4NH – ☎ (020) 7243 2201 – laccentorest@aol.com – £22-£28. Rustic surroundings and provincial, well priced, Italian cooking. Menu specialises in tasty pasta, made on the premises, and shellfish. Rear conservatory for the summer.

The Waterway – 54 Formosa St, Bayswater and Maida Vale, W9 2JU – ☎ (020) 7266 3557 – £15-£34.50. Pub with a thoroughly modern, metropolitan ambience. Spacious bar and large decked terrace overlooking canal. Concise, well-balanced menu served in open plan dining room.

N°.6 George St – 6 George St, Regent's Park and Marylebone, W1U 3QX – ☎ (020) 7935 1910 – £25.40-£32.95. To the front is a charming delicatessen offering fresh produce and behind is a simple, well-kept dining room. Daily changing menu with good use of fresh ingredients.

Al Duca – 4-5 Duke of York St, St James's, SW1Y 6LA – ☎ (020) 7839 3090 – info@alduca-restaurants.co.uk – £20.50-£24. Relaxed, modern, stylish restaurant. Friendly and approachable service of robust and rustic Italian dishes. Set priced menu is good value.

Olivo – 21 Eccleston St, Victoria, SW1W 9LX – ☎ (020) 7730 2505 – maurosanna@oliveto.fsnet.co.uk – £18-£27.50. Rustic, informal Italian restaurant. Relaxed atmosphere provided by the friendly staff. Simple, non-fussy cuisine with emphasis on best available fresh produce.

■ Further reading ■

Reference

AZ London Street Atlas
The Faber Book of London A N Wilson 1993
Georgian London John Summerson 1945 (1991)
The Blue Plaque Guide to London Caroline Dakers 1982
Notting Hill and Holland Park Past Barbara Denny 1993
The London Market Guide Metro Publications 1994
Access in London Couch Forrester and Irwin 1996
A History of London Stephen Inwood 1998
Writing London Julian Woolfreys 1998
A Literary Guide to London Ed Glinert 1998

Biography

The Shorter Pepys Robert Latham 1985
Diary John Evelyn 1818
Down and Out in Paris and London George Orwell 1933 (1982)
84 Charing Cross Road Helene Hanff 1978
In Camden Town David Thompson 1983
Three Men in a Boat Jerome K Jerome 1889
Longitude Dava Sobel 1996
London The Biography Peter Ackroyd 2000

Fiction

Our Mutual Friend Charles Dickens 1864/5
Picture of Dorian Gray Oscar Wilde 1891
The Adventures of Sherlock Holmes Arthur Conan Doyle 1892 (1993)
The Golden Bowl Henry James 1904 (1983)
Jeeves Omnibus P G Wodehouse
Mrs Dalloway Virginia Woolf 1925 (1972)
The Girl of Slender Means Muriel Spark 1963
Taste for Death P D James 1986
London Fields Martin Amis 1989 (1990)
The Secret Agent Joseph Conrad 1907 (1983)
The Buddha of Suburbia Hanif Kureishi 1990
Journal of the Plague Year Daniel Defoe 1722 (1992)
Liza of Lambeth W Somerset Maugham 1897
The Collected Stories of Muriel Spark 1994

■ Calendar of Events ■

Listed below are some of the most popular annual events. For specific dates and full details consult the national press and Tourist Information Centres.

January

Boat Show at Earls Court Exhibition Centre *(First Thursday)*
Start of Five-Nation Rugby Triple Crown at Twickenham
Charles I Commemoration held in Trafalgar Square

February

Chinese New Year in Soho
Clowns' Service at Holy Trinity, Dalston *(First Sunday)*

March

Chelsea Antiques Fair, Old Town Hall, Chelsea
Head of the River Race from Mortlake to Putney (420 crews leaving at 10 second intervals)
Oxford and Cambridge Boat Race from Putney to Mortlake

Easter

Service and distribution of Hot Cross buns at St Bartholomew-the-Great *(Good Friday)*
Carnival Parade in Battersea Park *(Easter Sunday)*
London Harness Horse Parade in Battersea Park *(Easter Monday)*
Kite Festival on Blackheath *(Easter weekend)*

April

RHS Spring Flower Show at Westminster
London Marathon from Docklands to Westminster

May

Royal Windsor Horse Show held in Home Park, Windsor
Chelsea Flower Show at the Royal Hospital, Chelsea
F A Cup Final
Chelsea Pensioners' Oak Apple Day Parade at the Royal Hospital, Chelsea *(29 May)*

June

Beating Retreat at Horse Guards Parade, Whitehall
Trooping the Colour at Horse Guards Parade *(Queen's Birthday)*
Hampton Court Music Festival at Hampton Court Palace

Spitalfields Annual Music Festival

Regent's Park Open Air Theatre Season

Stella Artois Grass Court (Tennis) Championships held at Queen's Club

Antique Fairs at Grosvenor House, Piccadilly and Olympia Exhibition Halls

Ascot Racing Week

British Polo Open Championships at Cowdray Park

Royal Academy Summer Exhibition at Burlington House, Piccadilly

All England Lawn Tennis Championships at Wimbledon *(2 weeks)*

Cricket Test Matches at Lord's and The Oval

Kite Festival on Blackheath *(last Sunday)*

July

Hampton Court Palace Flower Show

Royal Tournament at Earls Court

Sir Henry Wood's Promenade Concerts at the Royal Albert Hall *(8 weeks)*

Glyndebourne Opera Festival at Glyndebourne in Sussex

The City Festival is celebrated in the City Churches and Halls Swan Upping on the River Thames

Doggett's Coat and Badge Race rowed by 6 new freemen of the Watermen and Lightermen's Company from London Bridge to Chelsea Bridge

Opera and ballet at the Holland Park Outdoor Theatre

August

RHS Summer Flower Show in Westminster

Hampstead Heath Fair *(Bank Holiday Weekend)*

Notting Hill Carnival in Ladbroke Grove *(Bank Holiday Weekend)*

September

NatWest Trophy Final at Lord's Cricket Ground

Chelsea Antiques Fair held at Chelsea Town Hall *(First Saturday)*

October

Pearly Harvest Festival service for the Pearly Kings and Queens at St Martin-in-the-Fields *(First Sunday, afternoon)*

Goldsmith's Show, Goldsmiths Hall *(First week)*

Chelsea Crafts Fair held at Chelsea Town Hall *(two consecutive one-week shows)*

Opening of the Michaelmas Law Term: Procession of Judges in full robes carrying nosegays to Westminster Abbey

November

London to Brighton Veteran Car Run departing from Hyde Park Corner *(First Sunday)*

London Film Festival organised by the National Film Theatre *(three weeks)*
Lord Mayor's Show held in the City *(Saturday nearest to the 9th)*
Remembrance Sunday Cenotaph, Whitehall *(11am service; Sunday nearest 11 November)*
State Opening of Parliament by the Queen at Westminster
Regent Street Christmas lights are switched on

December

Lighting of the Norwegian Christmas Tree in Trafalgar Square
Carol Services throughout the capital's churches

INDEX